Surveys in Business and Economics 3

Banking Business Environment and Staff Performance

SURVEYS IN BUSINESS AND ECONOMICS

Series Editor

Wafik W.H. Kelliny

The goal of **SURVEYS IN BUSINESS AND ECONOMICS** is to address important topics meeting the needs of the growing number of business and economics scholars and professionals. Purposefully following a sequence from general principals to specific techniques, implementation strategies, and dissemination, the series volumes each examines interrelated aspects of business and economics. This comes in two forms, either a volume comprising a collection of edited papers by different authors, or a volume examining a particular aspect of business and economics research theme.

Volumes in the series:
1. **Surveys in Business and Economics 1:**
   Marketing and Human Resources across Cultures,
   By Wafik W.H. Kelliny
2. **Surveys in Business and Economics 2:**
   Perceptions of Organisations, Trainers and Employees
   of the Labour Market Needs
   By Wafik W.H. Kelliny and Salim Al Rizeiqi
3. **Surveys in Business and Economics 3:**
   Banking Business Environment and Staff Performance
   By Wafik W.H. Kelliny and Khalifa S. Al Said

Contributors may contact
the Series Editor:
kelliny@hotmail.com

Wafik W.H. Kelliny

and

Khalifa S. Al Said

Surveys in Business and Economics 3

Banking Business Environment and Staff Performance

First Published 2011
Series Editor: Wafik W.H. Kelliny
Charleston, SC
United States of America

British Library Cataloguing in Publication Data
    Surveys in Business and Economics 2
    - (Banking Business Environment and Staff Performance)
    Business Studies – Staff Appraisal, Banking and Business Environment
    I. Title   II. Series

ISBN   1451555105

Library of Congress Cataloguing in Publication Data
    Surveys in Business and Economics 2
    - (Banking Business Environment and Staff Performance)
    Business Studies – Staff Appraisal, Banking and Business Environment
    Bibliography: p.
    Includes indexes.
    Business Studies – Surveys. I. Title   II. Series

TABLE OF CONTENTS

ACKNOWLEDGEMENTS

We sincerely acknowledge the encouragement and support from many individuals and their organisations. Among those we would particularly express my gratitude to general managers, human resources and marketing managers and staff of the different national and international banks in Oman whom who provided us with their valuable information, comments and insights. Among these organisations Standard Chartered Bank, HSBC, Bank Beirut, Arab International National Bank of Oman, Oman Development Bank, Dhofar Bank, 'Bank Muscat', 'Bank Sohar', the Higher College of Technology, and the College of Banking and Financial Studies, Oman.

We also appreciate the valuable insights we received from David Harness, Susan Miller and Anna Snellen. Finally, we thank my colleagues who shared their experiences with me and contributed immensely with their views and suggestions on the volume.

Last but not least, Sultan Qaboos University, and the University of Lausanne and the University of Geneva, Switzerland, for their unconditional professional support.

INTRODUCTION

The banking industry is part of the backbone of the economy of every country. Oman is not exception to this. Six local and nine foreign banks are operating in Oman. They remain main source of employment for the majority of graduates coming out of the colleges and universities.

Banks carefully recruit employees and train them equally. The training given is independent of gender, caste, creed and background. But after the on the job-training, bank employees show different levels of performance. Their performance varies when they actually start to work in the different departments of their respective banks. The authors have observed that there are a number of factors that seem to play a negative role that the performance of bank employees, Omanis and expatriates alike.

The banking industry is undergoing lots of changes due to the turbulent world economy. For example, Lavender (2004) notes down some banks have been going through restructuring phases from time to time in the form of change of bureaucratic structure, e.g., selling everything from insurance to loans banking components. This is usually done to generate funds or to put an end to bank losses.

It is important that banks as well as their managers and personnel understand these changes and to develop their training programmes to meet the arising needs of the challenging business environment. This certainly will improve the productivity and performance of bank employees despite the changes occurring in this sector. As human resources are important for banks as well as other business organisations, the performance of the whole organisation depends on the quality of service and level of efficiency of its human resources. In so doing, banks as well as other organisations in Oman are expected not only to train Omanis, but also to transfer the needed skills and even professional attitudes and ethics for the best interest of the organisation and the Omani economy (Al Jabri, 2006; Al Lamki 1998, 1999 and 2000). Accordingly, banks and other organisations would be able to sustain competitive advantage (Porter, 1985; Barney, 1991) as human resources (HR) represent the core competence of the banking sector as well as other sectors (Collis, 1995; Prahalad and Hamel, 1990).

Accordingly, banks as well as other organisations not only ensure profitability, but also shape the future of the country and its economy (Bathmaker, 2005). Indeed, having a competitive edge and well trained personnel, which is the core competence of the banking industry, is needed today more than ever, taking into account the present dramatic collapse of the global banking industry. Indeed, well trained and well managed managers and staff represent the unique survival option that cannot be cloned by competitors.

Briefly, the purpose of this research project is to examine the factors that affect performance of bank employees. Accordingly, factors associated with better performance in drafting plans for monitoring and improving employee's performance are examined. This is done with the purpose of developing training programmes, providing guidelines to management in order to improve their organisations' performance and management level of efficiency and commitment. This is done by taking into account the following factors: knowledge and skills, performance appraisal and utilisation, remuneration, rewards and recognition, leadership and management, knowledge and skills of managers.

1   The Impact of Socioeconomic Background on the Banking Sector

1.1 The Impact of Socioeconomic Background on the Banking Sector

The Sultanate of Oman is a one of the Gulf States which maintains peaceful and healthy relations with the neighbouring nations. It is an active member in Gulf Council Countries (GCC). This council consists of UAE, KSA, Qatar, Kuwait and Bahrain. This GCC, which was formed in 1981, is one of the richest regions of the world with Gross Domestic Product (GDP) of US$324.36 billions (GCC Statistical Department, 2005).

Oman with an area of 309,500 sq km, UAE, KSA and Yemen are neighbouring countries sharing common borders. Oman is ruled by His Majesty Sultan Qaboos bin Said Al Said since 1970. Though there are no political parties in Oman, Majlis Al-Shura and Majlis Al-Dawla are the political representation system in Oman.

The people of Oman comprise two main groups: tribes and merchant families. The tribes are more in number in areas outside the capital, where as merchant families are situated in Muscat (EIU reports – Oman, 2006). Table 1.1 represents the population of Oman (Ministry of National Economy, 2006, p. 14)

Table 1.1: Population of Oman

Population(million) by Origin, 2006			
	Omani	**Non-Omani**	**Total**
Population	1.884	0.693	2.577

It is important to note that Oman has the majority of its population in the age group of 20-34 years old. It is believed that it brings uniqueness to Oman once the youth and potential human resources are well trained and their skills and potentials are used effectively. Table 1.2 classifies the population by age according to the latest census in 2006 (Ministry of National Economy, 2006, p. 14).

Table 1.2: Population by Age

Population by Age, 2006		
Age Groups	**No.**	**%**
Under 10 years	445,837	23.7
10-20 years	535,817	28.4
20-34 years	567,314	30.1
34-49 years	197,020	10.5
Over 49 years	137,588	7.3
Total	**1,883,576**	**100.0**

The economy of Oman is growing and maintains healthy status. The currency value is fixed against the US dollar and it is considered one of the most stable currencies in the Middle East. Oman ranks third in GDP, first and second being KSA and UAE respectively (Economist Intelligence Unit, Country Data, 2006).

Table 1.2: The Economy: Economic Structure

Main economic Indicators, 2007	
Real GDP growth (%)	5.3
Consumer price inflation (average %)	5.9
Current-account balance (US$ m)	4111.1
Exchange rate (average; OR:US$)	0.38
Population (m)	2.7
External debt (year-end; US$ m)	5,297.4

Table 1.3: Comparative Economic Indicators -2007

	Oman	Yemen	Saudi Arabia	Bahrain	UAE
GDP (US$ bn)	39.2	20.9	373.6	18.5	184.1
GDP per head (US$)	14,618	939	15,379	24,288	35,117
GDP per head (US$ at PPP)	22,619	2,218	23,099	32,102	27,933
Consumer price inflation (av. %)	5.9b	9.6	4.1b	3.6	14.0
Current-account balance (US$ bn.)	4.1	-0.5	91.9	2.1	31.6
Current-account balance (% of GDP)	10.5	-2.5	24.6	11.5	17.1
Exports of goods fob (US$ bn.)	22.9	7.1	230.0	13.4	156.6
Imports of goods fob (US$ bn.)	-11.0	-6.7	-81.2	-9.9	-101.6
External debt (US$ bn.)	5.3	6.0	52.1	7.9	57.5
Debt-service ratio, paid (%)	2.4	2.8	2.0	5.1	2.7

The economy of Oman is heavily dependent on hydrocarbons and contributes to 25% of GDP in real terms. But now Oman started showing concern in diversified projects. The diversification includes different sectors including LNG, gas-based industries etc. Tables 1.3 and 1.4 illustrate economic situation and economic indicators in comparison with other Middle East countries (Economist Intelligence Unit, Country Data, 2006).

1.2 The Banking Sector in Oman

As stated earlier, the banking sector maintains the financial equilibrium and economic stability of Oman. It consists of commercial and specialised banks, monitored and controlled by the Central Bank of Oman (CBO). Al Lamki (2005) has indicated that the banking sector of Oman is one of the oldest private sector establishments in Oman. She reiterates this from the fact of opening a branch of the British Bank of the Middle East in 1948. This sector is believed to contribute positively in the growth of the nation and cater to the needs of nation.

Table 1.4: Banking Sector of Oman

Banking Sector	2003	2004	2005	2006	2007
Number of Commercial banks	14	14	13	14	17
Number of branches of Commercial banks	327	330	329	338	362
Commercial Bank deposits (in RO million)	2853	3078	3761	4685	6491
Commercial Bank credit (in RO million)	3308	3506	3896	4703	6505
Number of cheques cleared (in 000)	1817	1772	1800	1873	2158
Average amount per cheque	1195	1240	1394	1496	1672
Reserve money (in RO million)	443	503	526	727	1235
Currency with public (in RO million)	304	329	383	471	563
Narrow money M1 (in RO million)	804	907	1128	1230	1921
Broad money M2 (in RO million)	2831	2944	3573	4461	6120
Ratio of NFA of CBO to Reserve money	3.1	2.7	3.2	2.7	3.0
Ratio of NFA of banking system to M2	0.5	0.6	0.6	0.6	0.6

The Central Bank of Oman is responsible for maintaining the value of the Omani Riyal (RO) and the financial system of Oman. The CBO started in 1975 with one million OR. Now its assets/liabilities come to around RO 1826.4 million (Oman Statistical Report, 2006). The CBO oversees bank deposits and insurance systems. It also warns early of any unforeseen financial crisis to its member banks. Its operations are mainly of two types: Direct and indirect measures to help the CBO in monitoring the financial instruments of the nation. Indirect monitoring includes securities, auctions, liquidity etc.; where as direct monitoring covers reserve requirements and lending ratios. Table 1.5 shows information about various banks in Oman and their financial status (CBO Annual Report, 2007, p. 17).

Table 1.5: Profiles of Banks

Type of Bank	Banks Date of Establishment	Local Branches
Local Bank 1	1975	82
Local Bank 2	1973	51
Local Bank 3	1973	28
Local Bank 4	1981	89
Local Bank 5	1990	43
Local Bank 6	1998	6
Local Specialised Bank 1	1977	9
Local Specialised Bank 2	1997	10
Local Specialised Bank 3	1997	7
Local Specialised Bank 4	1998	1
Foreign Bank 1	1948	7
Foreign Bank 2	1968	1
Foreign Bank 3	1972	11
Foreign Bank 4	1974	1
Foreign Bank 5	1975	1
Foreign Bank 6	1976	1
Foreign Bank 7	1976	3
Total		**351**

The specialist banks in Oman include several fields like housing, industry, fisheries and agriculture. Oman Development Bank (ODB) is responsible for housing loans for Omani citizens; and Oman Housing Bank (OHB) is responsible for subsidised and non-subsidised loans. This is according to the government directive from time to time, as they are the government specialised banks. The Alliance Housing Bank (AHB) is a private sector specialist bank. Table 1.6 shows the profiles of banks with the number of branches (CBO Annual Report, 2007, p. 17).

1.3   Human Resources and the Banking Sector

Before analysing the workforce in the banking sector, it becomes important to study the overall employment in Oman. Table 1.7 (CBO Annual Report, 2007, p. 19) shows the comprehensive data for employment in Oman. Table 1.8 is prepared exclusively for the banking sector, which reflects the numbers only in banking sector in Oman (Al Lamki, 2005, p. 176).

Table 1.6: Employment Scenario in Oman

Items	2003	2004	2005	2006	2007
Public Sector Employees	**123,045**	**127,121**	**132,414**	**138,806**	-
Omanis	99,076	104,223	109,424	116,054	–
Expatriates	23,969	22,898	22,990	22,752	–
Civil Service	*95,158*	*99,386*	*103,707*	*108,995*	–
Omanis	79,099	83,883	87,891	93,507	–
Expatriates	16,059	15,503	15,816	15,488	–
Diwan of Royal Court	*7,424*	*7,654*	*7,919*	*8,282*	
Omanis	4,573	4,764	5,010	5,261	–
Expatriates	2,851	2,890	2,909	3,021	–
Royal Court Affairs	*12,212*	*11,890*	*12,388*	*12,884*	–
Omanis	9,084	9,198	9,959	10,504	–
Expatriates	3,128	2,692	2,429	2,380	–
Public Corporations	*8,251*	*8,191*	*8,400*	*8,645*	–
Omanis	6,320	6,378	6,564	6,782	–
Expatriates	1,931	1,813	1,836	1,863	–
Private Sector Employees					
Omanis	74,816	87,064	98,537	114,311	131,775
Expatriates	407,168	424,319	424,788	510,713	638,447

It is also important to mention that the College of Banking and Financial Studies (CBFS), the Higher College of Technology and the other six Colleges of Technology in the different regions in Oman play a major role in preparing human resources for the banking sector. In addition to them, most of the graduates from Sultan Qaboos University and other various colleges also come to the human resources pool for the banking sector.

Table 1.7: Employment Scenario in Banking Sector

Year	1983	1985	1990	1995	2001
Omanis	1087	1635	2830	4080	4891
Non-Omanis	1630	1701	1047	647	504
Total Number of Employees	2717	3336	3877	4727	5395

Table 1.8: Distributions of Omani Personnel by Job Level in the Banking

Job level	Top and Middle Management	Clerical	Non-Clerical
Omani Personnel	82.50%	99%	100%

It is also important to note how the Omani personnel are distributed across various job levels. Almost 100% of non-clerical jobs are catered by Omani citizens, but in the higher level the percentage of the Omanis is decreased to 82.50%, as senior jobs are usually taken by expatriates, Table 1.9 (Al Lamki, 2005, p. 176). In addition, the distribution of gender among banking personnel in Oman's banking sector is also given in Table 1.10 (CBO Annual Report, 2007, p. 21) showing that more than two-thirds of the banking sector employees are males. However, one observes the opposite when he/she visits the 'front' offices and counters of the national and international banks in Oman.

Table 1.9: Distributions of Omani Personnel by Gender in Banks

Banks	Male	Female	Total
Local Bank 1	595	304	899
Local Bank 2	5583	292	875
Local Bank 3	351	140	491
Local Bank 4	896	537	1433
Local Bank 5	292	145	437
Local Bank 6	110	56	166
Specialised Bank 1	211	50	261
Specialised Bank 2	119	27	146
Specialised Bank 3	39	18	57
Specialised Bank 4	25	7	32
Foreign Bank 1	219	95	314
Foreign Bank 2	11	8	19
Foreign Bank 3	84	54	138
Foreign Bank 4	13	5	18
Foreign Bank 5	18	14	32
Foreign Bank 6	9	5	14
Foreign Bank 7	28	23	51
Total	**3603**	**1780**	**5383**

1.4 What does 'Performance' mean in the Banking Sector?

Like every organisation, performance is very important in the banking sector. In Oman various banks use different parameters to check the performance of their employees. As an example, if we take one of the leading banks in Oman, Bank Muscat carefully defines and measures performance of employees as its vision is to 'to satisfy one million customers in 2010'.

> "Our Quality Policy is to achieve and sustain a reputation for quality
> … Demonstrating vision, professionalism, transparency and integrity
> in the conduct of our business and service (p. 16). … Achieving
> disciplined growth and reasonable profitability while operating on a
> sound financial base (p. 14). … Creating value for our shareholders,
> encouraging, motivating and developing our human resources - our
> most valuable asset and the cornerstone of the bank (p.15).
>
> Bank Muscat (2006, pp. 14-16)

It is clear that Bank Muscat has realised the importance of HRM asset and carefully adopts the performance management right from its mission. In particular, on referring to their performance appraisal system, Bank Muscat annual report underlines that better performance means: "To get better results from employees and thereby achieving the bank's all business plans and objectives" (Bank Muscat, 2006, p.14).

The process of performance appraisal includes areas like self abilities, personal behaviour; execution of superior's instructions, innovation and working style. On the other hand, if we look at Standard Chartered Bank (SCB), it defines performance management and appraisal as "The process and behaviours by which managers manage the performance of their people to deliver a high-achieving organisation". At SCB they call an employee as best performing, when he or she helps in delivering the best from him and making the organisation a high achieving and competitive bank.

Accordingly, one may conclude that in general and in the service sector of banking in particular, a high performing employee is the one who:

- delivers good customer service.
- knows to maintain high quality required in the industry and on par with competitors.
- helps bank to achieve its objectives and goals.
- has potential self abilities, innovation and demonstrates good working style.
- helps in making the bank high achieving and highly competitive.

1.5 The 'Brain-Drain' Versus 'Novice' and Conclusion

The above data represent a clear trend in lower figures of Omani workforce in banks, in particular with the private sector banks. Public sector banks, according to the local government's principle decision, are seriously implementing Omanisation. Private sector banks without any such Omanisation requirements recruit personnel with state-of-the-art and talented people from the world labour market. But public sector banks are legislated to use local staff, characterising Omanisation.

During the interviews, one of the senior HR managers of the country, Mr. Sulaiman Al Hudaify of Oman Arab Bank, rightly points out the issue as follows:

> "We recruit young, un-trained diploma holders or graduates, train them with sector-specific focus. But despite this there is a 'brain-drain', switching over of the profession within a year - compelling us to go for recruitment and training exercise every year"

This poses two side threats to the banking sector. One is the sector itself is losing potential workers or it is becoming a less lucrative job/profession. The other one is the performance of a particular bank, which is facing the brain-drain and appointing novices and experiencing a disadvantage. In fact, it has been observed not only in Oman, but also in other Gulf countries; locals tend to change jobs seeking higher salary, senior position (without being ready for it, except being a local) or comfortable working hours. Loyalty or commitment usually goes to any or all these factors, rather than the organisation, regardless of the sector, which invests or is compelled to invest in training and developing the local staff. Some of the disadvantages of working for the banking sector as well as other private sector organisations are uncomfortable working hours, fewer holidays and unsecured jobs compared to working for the government or the public sector.

During the interviews, one of the HR managers of a leading private sector bank also indicated that:

> "We get efficient employees, with less salary and less incumbents comparing with his/her local counterparts, from countries like India. They can be trained and mended in the way we like. The existing stringent laws for expatriate labours do not allow smooth switch over of the job. Therefore, we have employees with years of experience, efficient and sincere minded"

Accordingly, banks encounter a serious problem in retaining their Omani staff with all possible risks. This is a great concern not only for the banking sector, but also for other sectors in the country which has an impact on its economy.

The ineffectiveness of employees negatively affects the profitability of the bank. Naturally, the nation's economy will suffer too. Therefore, banks should create a culture in their organisational system to ensure that each employee is personally and professionally loyal and committed to his profession as a banker.

Therefore, this study is expected to identify the causes of low performance of employees and to analyse how banks can retain trained employees and avoid the brain-drain phenomena of the Omani staff? Therefore, this study aims at helping banks as well as organisations in other sectors to improve the performance of their employees, retain employees and consequently have a competitive advantage by regarding its Omani staff as their lasting human asset. This is because expatriate staff, sooner or later, will have to be replaced by the Omanis.

2 HRM Models, Performance Management and Staff Appraisal

2.1 Introduction

The performance of every bank or any other service organisation depends on the quality of service given to the customers. Only a well-trained and quality workforce can deliver effective service in this highly competitive business, particularly in the middle of the worst recession the world is going through. Due to the difficulty in recruiting well trained human resources, particularly in developing countries or young nations, many of the banks are slowly losing many of their customers and even their brand names.

This study aims at proposing a human resources framework that can be used to monitor and manage change in employees' performance so as to improve the performance of banking professionals in Oman. Therefore, this chapter examines some of the most important factors that influence the performance of employee. The main focus is on:

- Examining the various conceptual frameworks and models which scrutinise the factors affecting motivation and performance.
- Human resources issues directly related to the banking sector.
- Perspectives on assessment and monitoring the performance of staff in different organisations.
- Management of competencies that guide and lead to performance improvement.

In other words, this chapter examines some of the challenges of HRM, with particular reference to service organisations. Then, it reviews some theoretical models and frameworks used in HRM. These include the 'matching model' and 'Harvard framework'. Though none of these models seems to fit entirely the case of the banking industry in Oman, each one seems to have some valid prospects for this sector. Therefore, this study presents a model, called a 'performance model', which has been synthesised and developed to be used in the banking industry in Oman and other service sectors as they share the same constraints of the prevailing business environment.

2.2 HRM: Challenges in Service Organisations

Human resource management is defined by Armstrong (2006) as the most valued asset which individually and collectively contributes to the achievement of the organisation's objectives. Storey (1992) views HRM as a punch of interrelated policies or rules with a philosophical and an ideological underpinning. Mathis and Jackson (2005) reinstate the central focus for HR management is on contributing to organisational success. They depict the key issues to enhance organisational performance by ensuring that human resources activities support organisational activities by focusing on productivity, service, and quality. This seems consistent to a great extent with the needs of the banking industry and its business environment in Oman. In every banking activity, one may find most of these management activities are interrelated or overlapping. Indeed, culture affects the banking industry in Oman, as well as in other parts of the world. The banking industry in Oman is as heterogeneous and multicultural as its population, as shown in Table 1.7. As a result, dealing with personnel, customers and staff who belong to different cultural backgrounds is part of the normal banking daily activities of both staff and management.

In other words, the business environment faced by HR management in the service sector is a challenging one; as changes usually occur rapidly across a wide range of issues. A study by the Judy and D'Amico (1997), entitled *Workforce 2020,* has highlighted some of the most important workforce issues. Mathis and Jackson (2005, pp 19-34) indicate that the most prevalent challenges facing HR management are as follows:
- Economic and technological change
- Workforce availability and quality concerns
- Demographics and diversity issues
- Organisational restructuring

Kinnie (2006) has elaborately discussed the challenges posed by the service industries to the HRM. He demonstrates this by showing the shift from agriculture to manufacturing and to service based economy of today's world. He also portrays that in all advanced industrial societies, the major employment depends on services. Briefly, the crucial feature of 'job' at the service sector can be described as intangibility, perishability or can not be stored; variability of the type quality of service because customers' role; simultaneous production and consumption; as well as inseparability or interaction between employee and customer. These variations of work at the service industry bring in following factors for HRM:

- Firms compete principally on the basis of their knowledge, both individually and collectively
- Valuable, rare, inimitable or cloned and non-substitutableaility to grow this knowledge and to grow it quickly can be a key source of a competitive edge in fast moving environments

Figure 2.1: Implications of HRM in the Service Sector

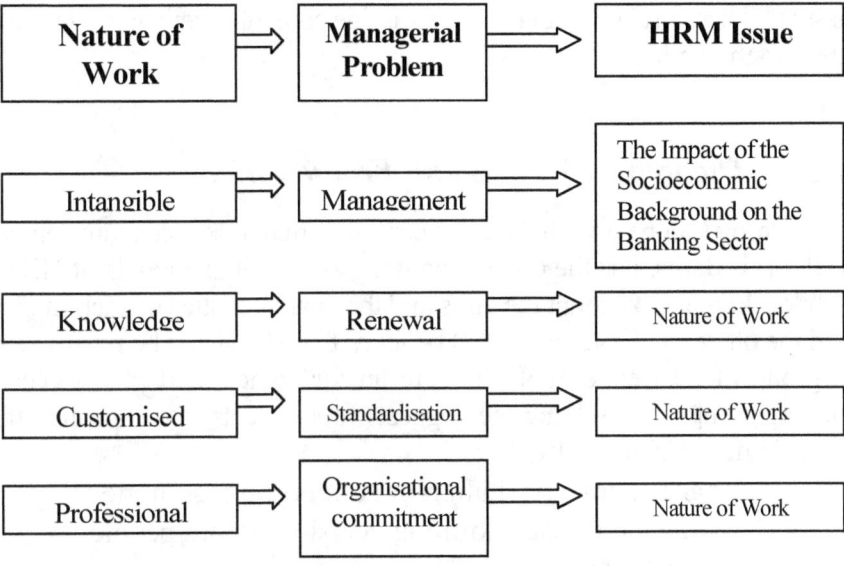

Kinnie (2006), in Figure 2.1, indicates that such differences in the varied nature work bring in various HRM issues which are associated with HRM in the service sector. Therefore, it is usually recommended that any HRM issues pertained to the service sector should be approached with the nature of work handled in contrast with the manufacturing industry.

The banking sector of Oman is no exception to this scenario of the service industry. The products/services that are being offered in a bank are actually intangible ones, and they have a great variance across the different segments and customers. What is described as a good service by one customer is unacceptable to another client. Though the management of the bank usually ensures quality transaction, the inseparable relationship between employees and customers decides the quality of the service/product. As Oman is a relatively small country, its economy is dependent to some extent on the US dollar prices. So, almost all the services of the banks in Oman come under the category of 'simultaneous production and consumption'. Kinnie (2006)'s implications of HRM in the service sector are recognised and accepted in detail in the Oman banking industry. Due to the intangible nature of the services offered in Oman's banking industry, they involve the complications from both managerial perspectives and related HRM issues. Therefore, it is essential to examine some theoretical models and their frameworks.

2.3   *Theoretical Models and Frameworks*

Armstrong (2006) says that the concept of human resource management (HRM) is defined as the one which integrates various models of HRM, while taking into account the aims and the characteristics of each model. On the other hand, Storey (1992) believes that HRM can be regarded as a group of interrelated policies with an ideological and philosophical underpinning. In so doing, he suggests four aspects that constitute the meaningful version of HRM:

- A particular constellation of beliefs and assumptions
- A strategic thrust informing decisions about people management
- The central involvement of line managers
- Reliance upon a set of 'levers' to shape the employment relationship.

2.4   Matching Model of HRM

One of the first explicit statements of the HRM concept was made by the Michigan School (Fombrun et al, 1984). They believe that HR systems and the organisation structure should be managed in a way that is congruent with organisational strategy (hence the name 'matching model'). They further explained that there is a human resource cycle (an adaptation of which is illustrated in Figure 2.2), which consists of four generic processes or functions that are performed in all organisations. These are:

- **Selection:** matching available human resources to jobs
- **Appraisal**: performance management
- **Rewards:** the reward system is the one which is the most under-utilised and mishandled managerial tool for driving organisational performance. It must reward short- as well as long-term achievements, bearing in mind that business must do well in the present to succeed in the future
- **Development:** developing high-quality employees.

Figure 2.2: Matching Model of HRM

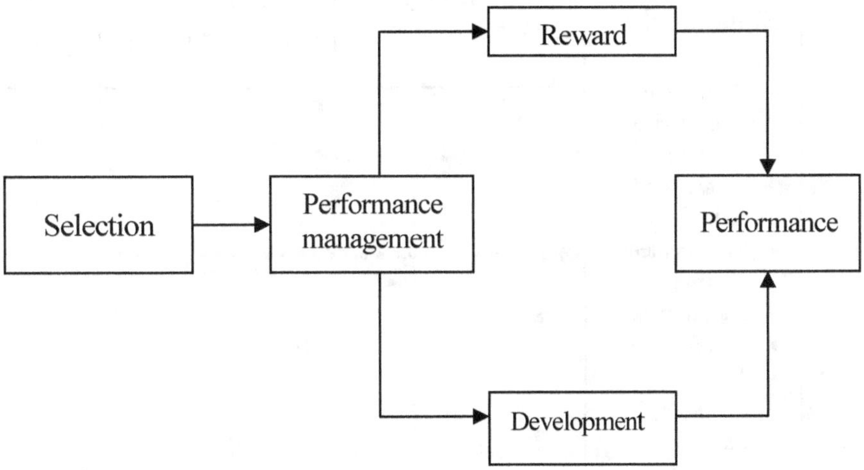

Fombrun et al.'s (1984, p. 4) concept is illustrated in Figure 2.2. However, the matching model does not correlate the performance with the stockholder's interests directly. To overcome this, the Harvard framework is suggested, see below.

2.5   Harvard Framework of HRM

The other founding fathers of HRM were the Harvard school's Beer et al. (1984), who developed the 'Harvard framework'. This framework is based on the belief that the problems of historical personnel management can only be solved.

Figure 2.3: Harvard Model of HRM

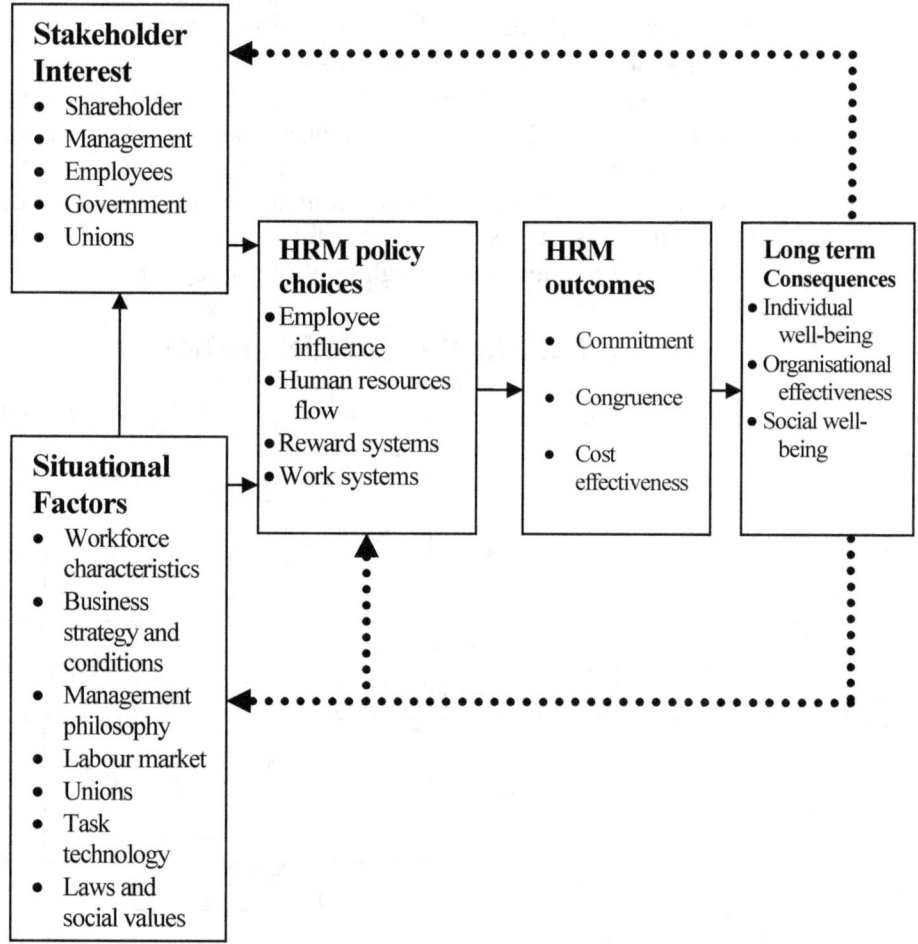

Beer and his colleagues believed that more focus on strategic perspective with regard to the organisation's human resources is needed to be able to encounter pressures of the business environment, particularly in the present devastating position of the banking sector all over the world. Beer et al. (1984) were the first to underline the HRM tenet that it belongs to line managers. They also emphasised the importance of human resource management as it involves all management decisions and actions that affect the nature of the relationship between the organisation, its staff or human asset and one may add, ultimately its customers.

Fombrun et al. (1984, p. 6) suggest that HRM has two characteristic features:
- Line managers who accept more responsibility for ensuring the alignment of competitive strategy and personnel policies;
- Personnel who have the mission of setting policies that govern how personnel activities are developed and implemented in ways that make them more mutually reinforcing.

Though the Harvard Model of HRM, Figure 2.3, is a developed version of the matching model, it does not include the productivity factor into the scenario of testing. As productivity is recognised as an important factor, employing it into the model will make it more applicable. This is done in the following performance model of HRM. This performance model is therefore developed and consolidated in a new version, at a later stage of this study.

2.6   *Performance Model of HRM*

Many factors can affect the performance of individual employees including their abilities, motivations, the support they receive, the nature of the work they are doing, and their relationship with the organisation. In many organisations, performance depends largely on the performance of individual employees. Robert et al. (2000; 2005) indicate that there are many ways to think about the kind of performance required of employees for the organisation to be successful; mainly Robert et al. (2000; 2005) focus on three key elements: productivity, quality, and service.

Organisational Effectiveness

The more productive an organisation, the better is its competitive advantage (Robert et al. 2000; 2005). This is because the organisation's costs to produce a unit of output are lower. Better productivity does not necessarily mean more is produced; perhaps fewer people (or less money or time) was used to produce the same amount. Mathis and Jackson (2005) mention a useful way to measure the productivity of a workforce is 'the total cost of people per unit of output'. Thus in its most basic sense, productivity is a measure of the quantity and quality of work done, considering the cost of the resources it took to do the work. It is also useful to view productivity as a ratio between input and output. This ratio indicates the value added by an organisation or in an economy.

Individual productivity
How a given individual performs depends on three factors: ability to do the work, level of effort and support given that person. Figure 2.4 (Mathis and Jackson, 2005, p. 76) illustrates these three factors.

Figure 2.4: Components of Individual Productivity

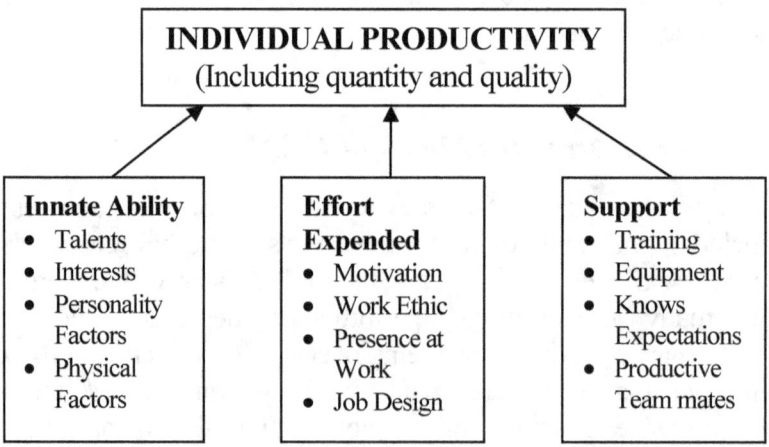

The relationship of these factors which widely acknowledged in management literature is that performance (**P**) is the result of ability (**A**) times effort (**E**) times support (S) (Mathis and Jackson, 2005, p. 81), as illustrated below.

$$P = A \times E \times S$$

Performance is diminished if any of these factors is reduced or absent. Recruiting and selection are directly connected to the first factor, innate ability, which involves choosing the person with the right talents and interests for a given job. The second factor, the effort exerted by an individual, is influenced by many HR issues, such as motivation, incentives, and job design. Organisational support, the third factor, includes training, available equipment, knowledge of expectations, and perhaps a productive team situation. HR activities involved here include training and development and performance appraisal.

Figure 2.5: Model of Individual/Organisational Performance

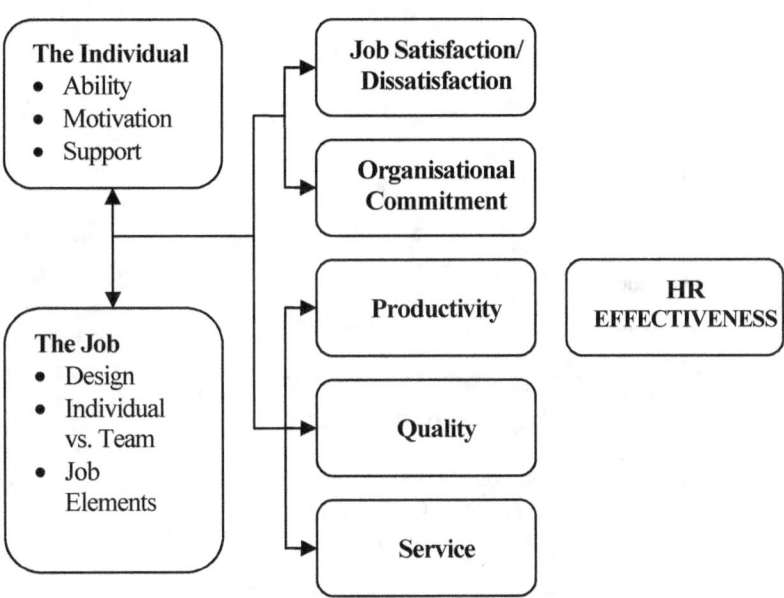

Mathis and Jackson (2005) suggest a model for individual/ organisational performance. This model shows the linkages, beginning with individual and job characteristics that lead to job satisfaction, organisational commitment, and affect the organisational outcomes: productivity, quality, and service. All five output variables, illustrated by Mathis and Jackson (2005), can be used to measure HR effectiveness. Sharpley (2002) proposed another effective model in contrast with what Robert et al. (2005). This is depicted in Figure 2.5 of Sharpley (2002, p. 18).

Figure 2.6: The Perception, Motivation and Performance Model

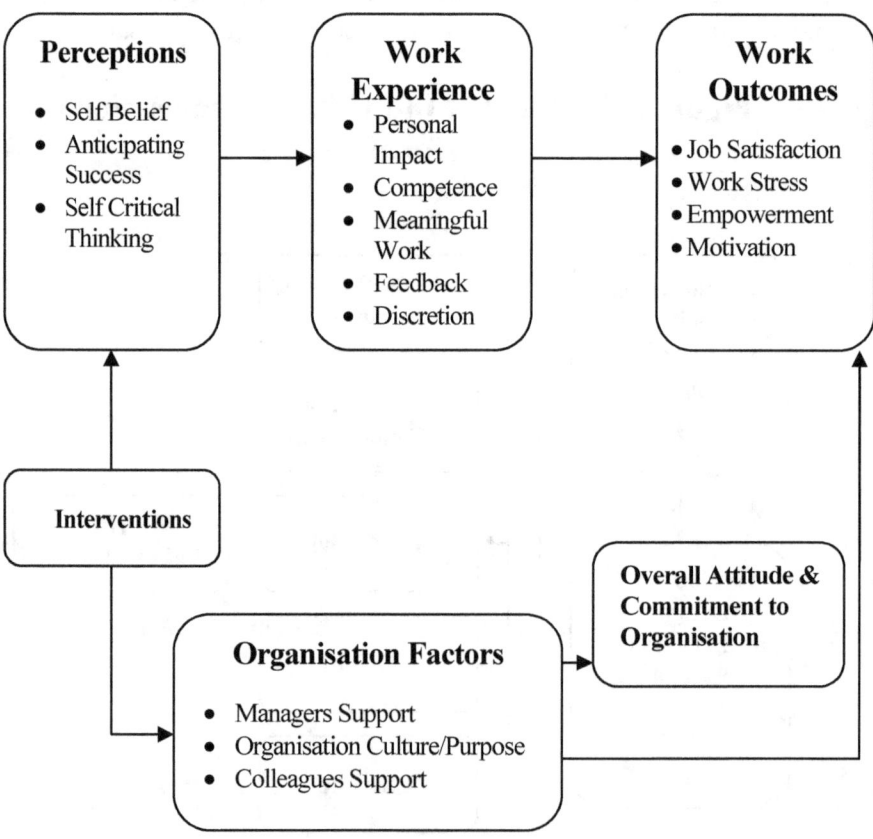

Sharpley (2002, p. 3), on the other hand, proposes another model, as depicted in figure 2.6, he identifies individual perceptions (self-belief, anticipating success and critical thinking), experience of work (personal impact, competency, meaningful work, feedback, and discretion) and work outcomes (job satisfaction, work stress, empowerment and motivation) as differences in individuals that affect their experience at work.

In addition, Sharpley (2002) adds more organisational factors such as managerial support; colleague support and organisational culture which are usually associated with high performance. Indeed, such interventions depend on the above mentioned factors, the attitude and commitment by the organisation which will eventually lead to the achievement of organisational goals.

Sharpley observes the individual differences through perceptions, experience and outcomes that are equally important like work motivation and positive performance. He further illustrates that these differences are linked to work demand. Only work demand, setbacks or disappointments will bring insight into issues that affect motivation and performance. Sharpley (2002, p. 24) highlights the most important aspect of maximum performance as the appreciation of one's role.

Nickols (2003, p. 28) outlines some factors which affect performance in the workplace. He emphasises that they are closely related performance factors:

- Clear goals
- Job expectations
- Suitable repertoire
- Immediate feedback
- Skills to perform
- Knowledge of the organisational structure
- Functional feedback system
- Sound mental models
- Sufficient motivation through self-satisfaction and incentives
- Supportive or conducive environment
- Manageable tasks.

By integrating Sharpley's model (2002) with Nickols' (2003), we can construct the following model which can be described as more complete and comprehensive, Figure 2.7. This developed model, called 'Performance Model' by Sharpley (2002) and Nickols (2003) is consistent with the performance requirement in the banking sector. This is because it contains most of the factors that have to be taken into consideration. Accordingly, this model has been used as a framework for the present study.

Oman's banking industry is undoubtedly highly influenced by social factors. This is because of relatively low population and close family and religious ties. It is almost true that in the capital banking sector almost all employees know each other. Just by seeing the name of an Omani, one can identify his family, sect and within few minutes almost every one will say, 'hey I know him or even her!' This is a closely related and religiously knitted society that puts more demands on the performance level of the HR resource.

As stated earlier, Oman's population has a large percentage of young people and families of many first generation graduates who join the banking industry. Therefore, in addition to the societal influence/ pressure, personal influence and individual perception put a great impact on one's performance. Organisations which are functioning on par with world class quality standards demand more output from these young Omanis, first generation college graduates of Oman. Their individual work experience and their performance at the workplace greatly influence their performance in general and in the banking sector in particular. Owing to the heterogeneous cultural workforce of Oman, one can not easily model this behaviour; instead all these factors may give a picture about the nature of the workforce and its performance in Oman.

2.7   *Performance Management*

What is performance management (PM)? There are many definitions. For example, Armstrong (2006) defines performance management as a systematic process for enhancing organisational performance by improving the performance of individuals and teams. Lockett (1992) also gives a definition but in a different way, as he defines performance management as developing individuals in terms of competence and commitment, working towards the realisation of shared meaningful goals and objectives within an organisation, which is characterised by supporting and encouraging its HR achievements.

The definition by Mohrman and Mohrman (1995) is more comprehensive and striking as it simply perceives performance management as a way to manage a business. This seems to have close link with the performance management in the banking industry. This is because the banking sector has to cater for the needs of both individual and commercial customers. Briefly, banking performance management is actually about helping customers to manage their businesses.

Cokins (2006) suggests that performance management is the framework for managing the execution of an organisation's strategy by indicating that PM is the way plans are transformed into results by integrating and developing usual business improvement methodologies with the use of technology.

In short, performance management is all about getting better results from the organisation, individuals and teams. It is a tool to check whether the organisation, teams and individuals have planned and shared goals and standards as well as different competencies in a multi-skilled organisation.

2.8   Aims of Performance Management

Armstrong (2006) indicates that the aim of such performance management is to establish a performing culture with individuals and teams, thereby dedicating to improvement of business processes. He also adds that the key purpose of performance management is to focus the individual on doing the right things through clear goals. IRS Employment Trends, in its August 2003 issue, categorised the aims of performance management system at various firms, Table 2.1 (IRS,, 2003, pp. 1-11).

Every bank in Oman is undoubtedly trying to provide quality services to their customer of different cultural backgrounds through the excellent performance of their employees. But how they manage and measure their employees' performance can easily be questioned. No doubt, such procedures will have an impact on the quality delivery to a great extent and in turn this will determine the success level of banks in Oman.

Table 2.1: Aims of Performance Management in World Leading Firms

No	Name of Firm	Aim
1	Armstrong World Industries	Empowering, motivating and rewarding employees to do their best.
2	Eli Lilly & Co	Focusing employees' tasks on the right things and doing them right. Aligning everyone's individual goals to the goals of the organisation.
3	ICI Paints	Proactively managing and assessing performance against agreed accountabilities and objectives.
4	Leicestershire County Council	Linking job performance to the achievement of the council's medium term corporate strategy and service plans.
5	Macmillan Cancer Relief	The alignment of personal/individual objectives with team, department/divisional and corporate plans. The presentation of objectives with clearly defined goals/targets using measures, both soft and numeric. The monitoring of performance and tasking of continuous action as required.
6	Marks & Spencer Financial Services	All individuals being clear about what they need to achieve and expected standards, and how that contributes to the overall success of the organisation; receiving regular, fair, accurate feedback and coaching to stretch and motivate them to achieve their best.
8	Standard Chartered Bank	The process and behaviours by which managers manage the performance of their people to deliver a high-achieving organisation.

2.9 Characteristics of Performance Management

Performance management is about giving managers and employee teams of all levels the capability to improve their organisation's direction, traction, and speed, and most important, to move it in the right direction. That direction should be as clear and focused as a laser beam, pointing toward its defined strategy (Cokins, 2006).

The process of managing strategy begins with focus. Armstrong (2006) divides it into five integral parts, which are: agreements, measurement, feedback, positive reinforcement and dialogue. The following are the characteristics of performance management:

1. Performance management is a process which is continuous and flexible. It involves managers and partners to set out how they can best work together to achieve the required results.

2. It is based on the principle of management by contract and agreement and not through management by command. It relies on consensus and cooperation rather than control or coercion.

3. Performance management focuses on future performance planning and improvement rather than on retrospective performance appraisal. It functions as a continuous and evolutionary process, in which performance improves over time; and provides the basis for regular and frequent dialogues between managers and individuals about performance and development needs.

4. It is mainly concerned with individual performance but it can also be applied to teams. The focus is on development, although performance management is an important part of the reward system through the provision of feedback, recognition and the identification of opportunities for growth.

5. It may be associated with performance- or contribution-related pay, but its developmental aspects are much more important (Armstrong, 2006).

All these above-mentioned characteristics are seamlessly seen in Oman's banking sector. All the banks have understood the importance of performance management in principle and this is evident through bankers' attention in this area.

2.10   Performance Appraisal

Table 2.10: Performance Appraisal Framework

Phase	Activity	Typical Procedure
I	*Performance Planning*	• At the beginning of the year, the manager and individual get together for a performance-planning meeting. • In this hour-long session, they discuss what the person will achieve over the next twelve months and how the person will do the job.
II	*Performance Execution*	• Over the course of the year, the employee works to achieve the goals, objectives, and key responsibilities of the job. • The manager provides coaching and feedback to the individual to increase the probability of success. • He/she creates the conditions that motivate and resolves any performance problems that may arise.
III	*Performance Assessment*	• As the time for the formal performance appraisal nears, the manager reflects on how well the subordinate has performed over the course of the year, assembles the various forms and paperwork that the organisation provides to make this assessment, and fills them out. • The manager may also recommend a change in the individual's compensation based on the quality of the individual's work. • The completed assessment form is usually reviewed and approved by the appraiser's boss, others, perhaps the department.
IV	*Performance Review*	• The manager and the subordinate meet, usually for about an hour. They review the appraisal form that the manager has written and talk about how well the person performed over the past twelve months. • At the end of the review meeting, they set a date to meet again to hold a performance-planning discussion for the next twelve months, at which point the performance management process starts a new cycle.

Figure 2.7: Performance Appraisal Framework

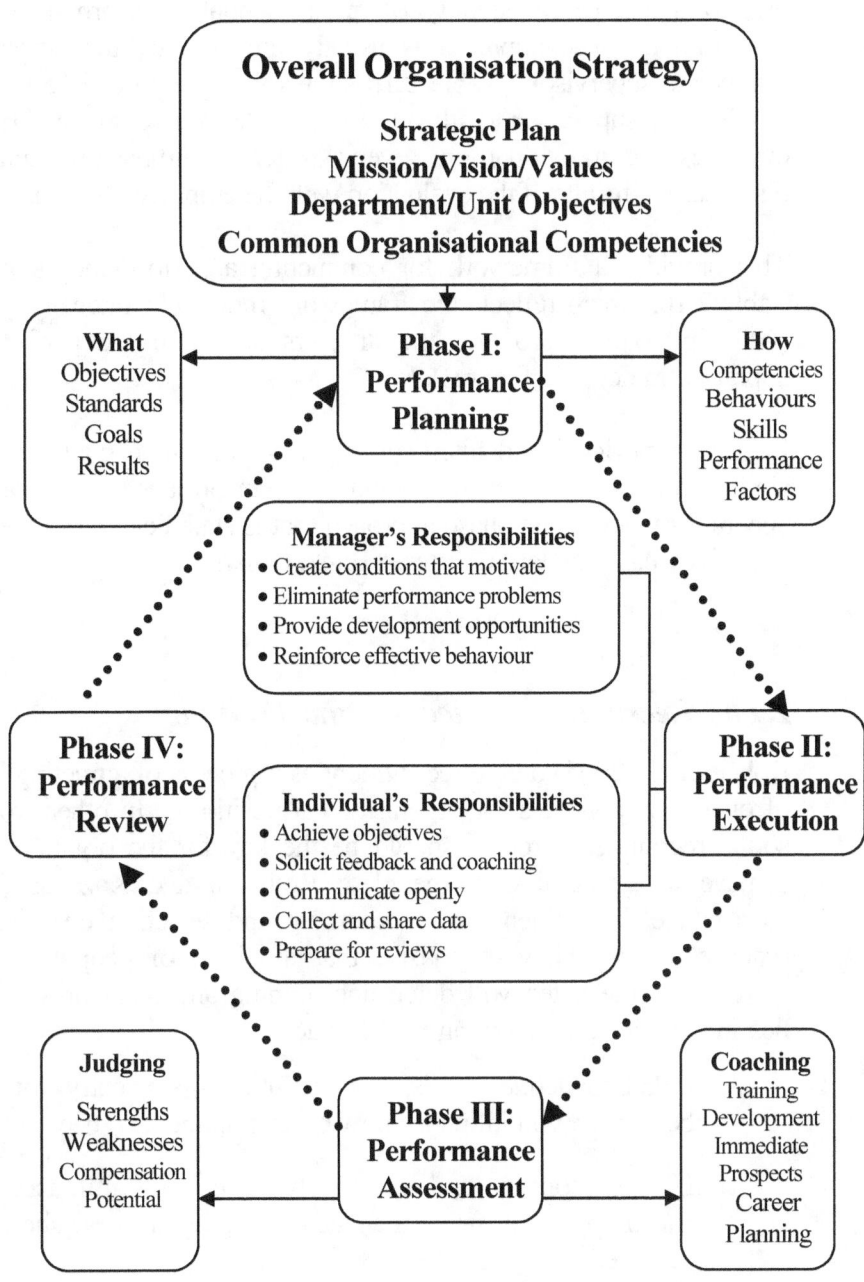

Overall Organisation Strategy

**Strategic Plan
Mission/Vision/Values
Department/Unit Objectives
Common Organisational Competencies**

What
Objectives
Standards
Goals
Results

**Phase I:
Performance
Planning**

How
Competencies
Behaviours
Skills
Performance
Factors

Manager's Responsibilities
• Create conditions that motivate
• Eliminate performance problems
• Provide development opportunities
• Reinforce effective behaviour

**Phase IV:
Performance
Review**

Individual's Responsibilities
• Achieve objectives
• Solicit feedback and coaching
• Communicate openly
• Collect and share data
• Prepare for reviews

**Phase II:
Performance
Execution**

Judging
Strengths
Weaknesses
Compensation
Potential

**Phase III:
Performance
Assessment**

Coaching
Training
Development
Immediate
Prospects
Career
Planning

Performance appraisal is a formal management system that provides for the evaluation of the quality of an individual's performance in an organisation. The appraisal is usually prepared by the employee's immediate supervisor. Table 2.10 shows that the procedure typically requires the supervisor to fill out a standardised assessment form that evaluates the individual on several different dimensions and then discusses the results of the evaluation with the employee (Grote, 2002).

This provides a framework for conducting a performance appraisal, Table 2.10, which reflects the framework more schematically. Grote (2002, p. 3) also provides the different stages of the performance appraisal framework, Figure 2.7.

In fact, some local and international banks in Oman claim to use a similar methodology in managing the performance appraisal that encompasses the three phase approach that is stated clearly in the bank objectives, e.g. Standard Chartered Bank, Oman.

2.11   Recruitment, Selection and Training

Robert et al. (2005) define recruitment as a process of attracting a pool of qualified applicants for organisational positions. In other words, a sound recruitment process should be the key for the organisation to achieve its goals, through people. Rothwell and Kazanas (2003) substantiate the influence of recruitment and selection on other HR practice areas. They emphasise that the kind of people who are recruited and selected will determine training and other programmes, bearing in mind the following HRM issues:

1. HR knowledge, skills, and abilities upon entry, or entry behaviour, will influence how much training they need.

2. HR self-concept and career objectives will influence what career planning and management programmes should be designed.

3. HR attitudes and interpersonal skills will influence what organisational development efforts need to be made in order to improve work-group relations.

4. HR individual values and abilities will influence job design (the reason is that people will try to personalise their jobs, reshaping work requirements to fit their skills and perhaps even their interests).

5. HR individual abilities to deal with job-induced stress and personal problems can affect their need for the 'employee assistance programme.'

6. HR perceptions about labour unions, which is not applicable in Oman, can influence potential for unionisation.

7. HR individual desires and expectations can influence appropriate compensation needed to reward, retain, and motivate personnel.

Table 2.11: Internal Versus External Recruitment

	Advantages	Disadvantages
Internal	• Morale of promotee • Better assessment of abilities • Lower cost for some jobs • Motivator for good performance • Causes a succession of promotions • Have to hire only at entry level	• Inbreeding • Possible morale problems of those not promoted • 'Political' fighting for promotions • Need for management-development programme
External	• New "blood" brings new perspectives • Cheaper and faster than training or organisation professionals • No group of political supporters in organisation already • May bring new industry insights	• May not select someone who will "fit" the job • May cause morale problems for internal candidates not selected • Longer "adjustment" or orientation time

Recruitments can be done internally or from external labour markets. Mathis and Jackson (2005, p. 252) compare and contrast internal and external market recruitments, Table 2.11.

Figure 2.8: Recruiting Decisions

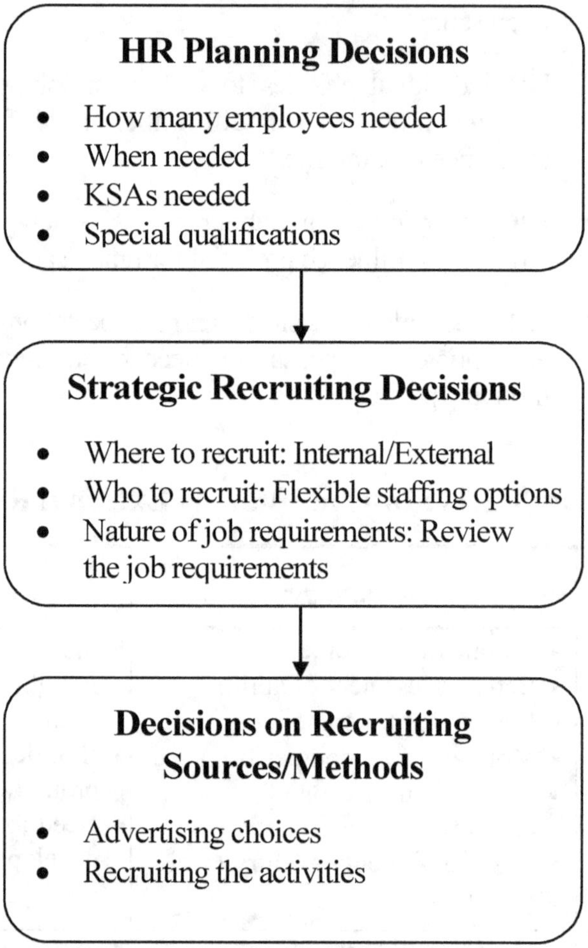

```
┌─────────────────────────────────────────┐
│           HR Planning Decisions          │
│                                          │
│   •  How many employees needed           │
│   •  When needed                         │
│   •  KSAs needed                         │
│   •  Special qualifications              │
└─────────────────────────────────────────┘
                     │
                     ▼
┌─────────────────────────────────────────┐
│        Strategic Recruiting Decisions    │
│                                          │
│   •  Where to recruit: Internal/External │
│   •  Who to recruit: Flexible staffing   │
│      options                             │
│   •  Nature of job requirements: Review  │
│      the job requirements                │
└─────────────────────────────────────────┘
                     │
                     ▼
┌─────────────────────────────────────────┐
│          Decisions on Recruiting         │
│               Sources/Methods            │
│                                          │
│   •  Advertising choices                 │
│   •  Recruiting the activities           │
└─────────────────────────────────────────┘
```

Mathis and Jackson (2005, p. 73) also describe steps needed in making recruitment decisions like recruitment from internal or external pool of candidates, Figure 2.8. Selection is indeed a very important area where decisions contribute to the success of the organisations. There are many methods available for selecting an employee. Figure 2.9 outlines various tests which are available.

Figure 2.9: Possible Tests Used for Selection

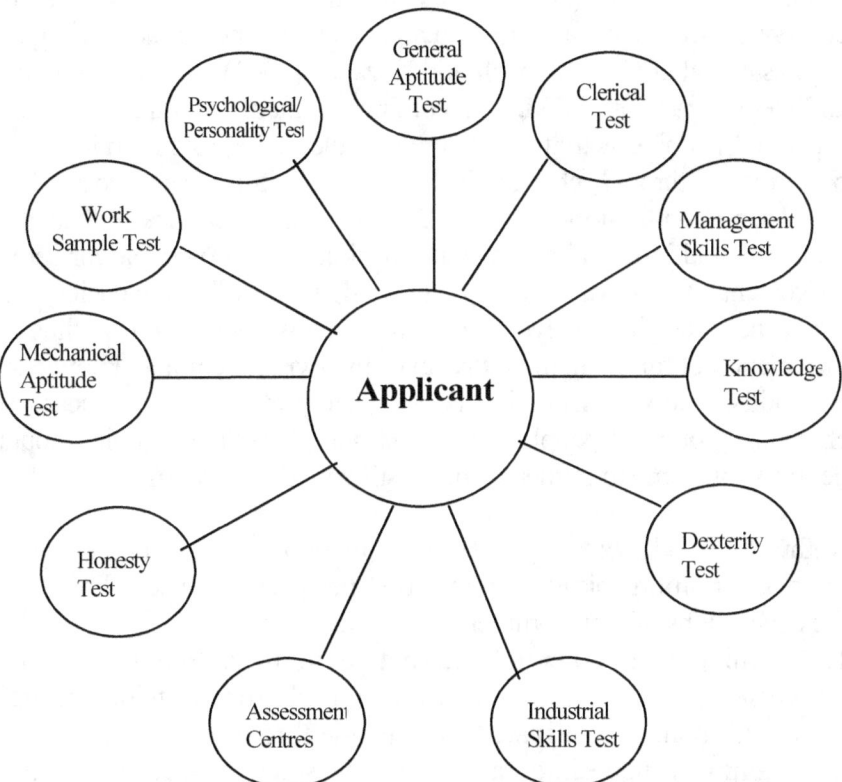

The different types of tests include some of the types/elements listed below, which are also summarised in Figure 2.9 (Mathis and Jackson, 2005, p. 293).

- Ability tests assess the skills that individuals have already learned.
- Aptitude tests measure general ability to learn or acquire a new skill.
- Mental ability tests measure reasoning capabilities.
- Some of the abilities tested include spatial orientation, comprehension and retention span, as well as general and conceptual reasoning.
- The General Aptitude Test Battery (GATB) is a widely used test of this type.

After recruitment the other area which is important in HRM is training. Mathis and Jackson (2005) define training as the process whereby employees acquire capabilities and abilities to help towards realising the organisational goals. Rothwell and Kazanas (2003) add that training is an integral part of HRM. According to them, training comprises organised learning activities that are capable of improving individual's performance through changes in knowledge, skills, or attitudes. In a broad sense, on-the-job-training (OJT) includes experiences intended to meet essential job requirements, update skills, prepare people for career movement of any kind, rectify knowledge or skill deficiencies, and evoke new insights or even create new knowledge. OJT is thus an important tool for changing individuals by giving them new knowledge and skills. However, training is not usually effective as a means of changing groups of people, since it is rarely possible to train enough people at one time to influence the existing work environment.

Rothwell and Kazanas (2003) have mentioned the importance of training for an organisation from HRM perspective. The following is the conclusions of their comments about training:
1. Training is a potential alternative to recruitment, and vice versa. Needed skills can be acquired from outside through recruitment, or cultivated from inside through training.
2. Training can be integrated with the selection process so that an employee's learning time on a new job is reduced. The result should be increased level of efficiency.
3. Training can admittedly increase the risk of turnover (which is a problematic issue when recruiting and investing in the training of Omani employees), especially when it builds skills transferable from one job to jobs in other organisations.
4. Training is a vehicle for career progress that can help move people in a way that is consistent with their career plans and/or the career management programmes of the organisation.
5. Training tends to build expectations for change, and thereby helps foster new attitudes. It thus influences organisation development efforts and can be used as a constructive tool.
6. Training builds skills and can thus influence, and be influenced by, job redesign initiatives that might depend on the range of skills possessed by job incumbents.

7. Training can convey information about how to deal with personal/family problems, which are common in the Omani context. It thus serves to change the behaviour of supervisors when they encounter "problem employees." In this way, training can influence employee assistance programmes.

   a. Training can increase individual productivity by giving employees skills they did not have before. Such productivity improvement efforts are generally opposed by unions, which is so far not the case in the Omani context, unless they are accompanied by corresponding increases in pay and job security. On the other hand, unions typically support upgrading skills so that people stay current and occupationally mobile.
   b. Training can create the expectation for increasing compensation and benefits, as employees improve their productivity and knowledge, which is generally ignored by most public and private sector employers.

2.12   HRM Issues in the Banking Sector

Briefly, most of the studies on motivation in the banking sector have concluded that:
- The banking sector has the most motivated workers in comparison with other service sectors and industries.
- Banking staff valued individual development, team work and job tasks.
- People working in the banking sector are usually better at work and they usually work harder than others in other sectors.

The following factors generally affect motivation:
1. To be treated fairly
2. To have the salary related to performance
3. To be able to affect work outcome
4. To get respect related to performance
5. To get support from the boss
6. To have an interesting job

7. To be safe at work
8. To have a good relation with the boss
9. To participate in the goal formulation
10. To develop
11. To get feedback from the boss
12. To be rewarded in relation to performance
13. To have suitable rewards
14. To have responsibility
15. To feel a belonging to the co-workers
16. To feel a belonging to the organisation
17. To receive appreciation from the co-workers

Lavender (2004) has shown clearly that the changing environment in the bank made the workers undergoing lots of trouble. Hunter and Thatcher (2007) discuss such issues with bank employees in depth. They find there are two factors contributing to this problem. One is the structure that brings complacencies and the other is fast changes that are taking place in banks. Hunter and Thatcher add further that these changes bring unpleasant working conditions and put employees in trouble through pressurising them.

Smith *et al.* (2000) insist that it is the sales goals that put employees in trouble and they quote further that such goals lead to decreasing employees' motivation. But that may encourage unethical behaviour through manipulation of statistics or balance sheets. Whitaker (2007) took the case of Standard Chartered Bank and proved that only committed employees contribute to the company's profit.

Wilkinson (1995) illustrates that the changing nature of banking have a 'knock-on' effect on HRM, particularly in employee relations. He also demonstrates that banks have started moving towards market driven culture and should start recognising staff as resource than a cost. These findings are found with the reflections mentioned in each section relevant to the banking scenario in Oman's banking sector. All these factors found during this literature review are indeed applicable in the case of the banking arena in Oman.

2.13 Conclusion: Staff Development and Appraisal

Banks, being a service sector, necessarily pose special challenges to the HRM issues and thus the identified challenges can be applied to the present case study. In order to find the factors affecting the performance of bank professionals, both positively and negatively, it is found that various models of HRM can help in answering the raised questions. Some of the HRM models were reviewed including the Matching Model, Harvard Model and Performance Model. It was then concluded that the Performance Model addresses the present problem chosen in the study. Sharpley (2002) and Nickols (2003) describe the performance model by keeping the factors affecting the performance as the basic theme behind it. Therefore, it was found appropriate to use such a model to see whether the requirements are met to get the maximum performance from the study sample of the banking sector employees. This will help to realise the main objective of the study, i.e. identifying the factors affecting performance in the banking sector in Oman.

In order to focus other research questions related to facilitating good performance, a section in the literature review was allotted to performance management. In this section, the literature pertaining to aims of the performance management and performance appraisal was reviewed. Armstrong (2006) and Lockett (1992) definitions emphasise the broad meaning and outreach of performance appraisal. This section also revealed the importance of managing performance before expecting them from the employees. The framework recommended by Grote (2002) for the performance appraisal was found effective in the local Omani perspective. This is in answer to the second objective of the study, i.e. whether the employees' performances are properly appraised or not, and rewarded accordingly or not.

To answer the third research question 'strategies to increase performance of employees', the remaining part of literature review focussed on recruitment, selection, and training and then characteristics features of service sector's HRM issues. While focussing on recruitment, selection and training, it was revealed that they are vital for organisational HRM. Methods of recruitment and steps in selecting the right calibre of employees were discussed. Rothwell's and Kazanas' (2003) views which focussed on training as effective means to meet

HRM objectives were also examined. This is expected to address the third problem, i.e. to ensure employees are performing well and achieving organisational objectives. Mathis' and Jackson's (2005) view of key steps in recruitment decisions were synthesised as an important framework for the purpose of this study. The human capital acquired through the recruitment, selection and training naturally ensures that employees support the strategy of the bank and attract a 'performance pool' of multi-skilled and motivated employees.

In the last section, HRM issues pertaining to the banking industry were also reviewed. This highlighted the fact of the changing nature of the banking environment, thus making HRM a complicated mission. This has also revealed that banking employees are particularly lacking in motivation. In particular, Hunter's and Thatcher's (2007) findings revealed complications in organisational structure that were attributed to unpleasant working conditions. Kirk Smith *et al.* (2000) insisted that the goals set by the bank bring down the motivation of the employees. Whitaker (2007) who studied the Standard Chartered Bank concluded that only commitment of the worker will bring better work performance.

Accordingly, staff development and appraisal should be aligned with the bank's goals and strategies leading to well trained, loyal and committed staff. This can be realised in developing a training programme. So, the observations and understanding of the performance appraisal process should help to reduce a monumental task into something much more manageable.

Briefly, the term performance appraisal has been called by many names, including performance review, performance evaluation, personnel rating, merit rating, employee appraisal or employee evaluation. A performance appraisal can be defined as any personnel decision that affects the status of an employee regarding their retention, termination, promotion, transfer, salary increase or decrease, or admission into a training programme.

Training Programme Objectives
At the end of the training programme, staff should be able to:
   1. Translate organizational goals into individual job objectives

2. Communicate management's expectations regarding employee performance
3. Provide feedback to the employee about job performance in light of management's objectives
4. Coach the employee on how to achieve job objectives/ requirements
5. Diagnose the employee's strengths and weaknesses.
6. Determine what kind of development activities might help the employee better utilize his or her skills to improve performance on the current job.

The content of the programme should lead to:
1. Providing employees the opportunity to formally indicate the direction and level of the employee's ambition
2. Showing organisational interest in employee development, which was cited to help the enterprise retain ambitious, capable employees instead of losing the employees to competitors
3. Providing a structure for communications between employees and management.
4. Providing satisfaction and encouragement to the employee who has been trying to perform well
5. Enhancing the ability to promote, separate and transfer decisions
6. Feedback to the employee regarding how the organization viewed the employee's performance
7. Evaluations of relative contributions made by individuals and entire departments in achieving higher level organization goals
8. Having clear criteria for evaluating the effectiveness of selection and placement decisions, including the relevance of the information used in the decisions within the organization
9. Making reward decisions, including merit increases, promotions, and other rewards
10. Ascertaining and diagnosing training and development decisions
11. Developing objective and realistic criteria for evaluating the success of training and development.

3 Qualitative and Quantitative Research Methodology

3.1 Research Design and Study Objectives

The present study was undertaken according to a quantitative research model with an explorative and descriptive design. It is because a quantitative process will allow collecting numerical data that will enable us in experimental and quasi experimental approach. Descriptive research is expected to bring in new knowledge about the subject, situation and the frequency of certain phenomena. Burns and Grove (1993) too illustrates that descriptive research will lead to exploration and description in real situations.

Such exploratory design necessitates the use of questionnaires, a quantitative instrument, to sample the population. Such use of a questionnaire helped the writers in finding facts related to the field of study and to peep into the depth of the study, including its manifestation and related factors.

Therefore, this study incorporates the survey method of data collection to reach bank employees of different and distant branches. This survey method permits the absence of the writers. As it can be done in the absence of the researcher, it may remove biasing or misquotation of the questionnaire. However, the authors went individually to some banks/branches seeking clarifications from the available managers and staff, following the analysis of the data that was collected through the questionnaires.

The entire approach is led by the problem statement of this research with main objective of identifying any gap in the knowledge. The problem statement will, therefore, articulate the nature, context and significance of the study.

The present study was based on two criteria:
- Firstly, the factors that affect performance of bank employers were to be determined in relation to human resources

management activities, with a focus on the service sector in Oman.

- Secondly, two groups of banks, national and international, were selected. One group had more than 1000 customers per branch and the other had less than 1000 customers.

3.2   *Study Questions*

1. To what extent does human resources management affect the performance of bank employees in Oman, regardless of their banks' size?

2. Do the human resources management styles affect the banks in Oman and in turn the Omani economy?

3. Do the Omani banks take into account the human resources management factors including:

    - knowledge and skills,
    - performance appraisal and utilisation,
    - remuneration,
    - rewards and recognition
    - leadership and management, and
    - knowledge and skills of managers?

3.3 *Hypothesis of the Study*

The study null hypothesis is as follows:

"Human resources management factors, including knowledge and skills; performance appraisal and utilisation; remuneration; rewards and recognition; leadership and management; as well as knowledge and skills of managers, do not affect the performance of bank employees."

3.4   Study Sample

In this particular study, 'stratified random sampling' is used because all bankers can be classified into two 'strata'. One is professional bankers, who meet the customers and transact their orders that are referred to as subordinates.   The other one is supervisors or those holding management positions that are referred to as bank managers.

The target population for this study is all the banking professionals working in leading national and international banks in Oman. They are six local banks, four national banks and four foreign/international banks, including: Standard Chartered Bank, HSBC, Bank Beirut, Arab International National Bank of Oman, Oman Development Bank, Dhofar Bank, 'Bank Muscat', 'Bank Sohar'. They are about 5383 employees on the payroll. The employers and managers of these selected banks/branches were requested to participate in the study. Table 3.1 shows the population and number of samples chosen.

Table 3.1: Gender Distribution of Managers and Non-Managers of the Study Sample

	Managers		Sub-ordinates		Total
Category	Male	Female	Male	Female	
Number	114	66	264	276	720
%	63.3	36.7	48.9	51.1	100/100

Burns and Grove (1993) demonstrated that a mere 10% of sample is sufficient to control any sampling errors that may creep in.   This selected sample percentage is well above 10 % and therefore it is expected to provide a true representation of population. Accordingly, a simple random sampling was used. The following steps were followed in order to do this:

- A latest, up-to-date staff list was obtained from the bank/branch.
- Two lists with numbers were made, one for managers and another one for bank staff.
- Any staff or manager who was on leave was removed from the list.
- With the help of random numbers, the required number of staff and managers were selected.

3.5   Test Instruments

A) Design of the Questionnaires

The content of the two questionnaires were planned in such a way that the posed research question, aided with the findings of the literature review, is taken in the instrumentation of the questionnaire. For this purpose, two questionnaires were designed.

a. The objective of the first questionnaire was to identify the factors that affect the performance of bank staff both positively and negatively. It also focused on strategies to improve their performance, Appendix A.

b. The second questionnaire aimed at identifying the skills and competencies of bank managers in order to facilitate improved performance by their subordinates, Appendix B.

The two questionnaires were designed in accordance with the objective and the research questions of the present study, and conclusions from the literature review on performance model, recruitment and selection, and HRM issues in service industries.

Table 3.2: Content of the Questionnaires

Content	Questionnaire	
	I (Appendix A)	**II (Appendix B)**
Section A: Personal Information	1 to 4	1 to 4
Section B: Organisational details	5 to 8	5 to 8
Section C: Knowledge and HRM issues	9 to 19	9 to 19
Section D: Organisational Processes	20 to 59	20 to 59

As explained above, there were two planned questionnaires. Each questionnaire was divided into four sections. The first section was to identify the personal information like age, gender, qualification and experience. The second section was aimed mainly at describing the nature of employment in the respondents' organisations, departments, and work environment. The third section was to identify the employees' knowledge and the skills. This section contained issues discussed in the literature review about the performance management and training (Armstrong, 2006). This section also focussed on staff motivation. The fourth section dealt with the organisational processes. These questions were expected to bring out the problems in accordance with the performance model by Sharpley (1984). Table 3.2 identifies the main themes of the two questionnaires, Appendix A: "Questionnaire for Banking Staff", and Appendix B: "Questionnaire for Banking Managers."

B) Interviews

Due to the limitations of the questionnaire as a testing instrument, it was deemed essential to use interviews. This is because a questionnaire as a data collection tool has a limited scope; in other words, some important information/questions might be missed or ignored either during the development or the validation of the questionnaire. Due to cultural factors, participants were likely to avoid expressing their views and facts 'in writing'. On the other hand, during the interviews more data was collected and other avenues emerged to be explored more freely. The interviews mainly addressed the issues raised in the two. Furthermore, the free nature of interviews has resulted in collecting a wider range of data, more than the expected answers in response to Appendices A and B.

C) Observations

Observations were also a useful in helping to integrate and analyse the overall results.

D) Materials and documents

Documents and data from the banks, ministries and government bodies including Standard Chartered Bank, Oman, Bank Muscat, Oman, the Ministry of National Economy and the Chamber of Commerce, the Ministry of Manpower were also collected to support or discredit the collected data, mainly the qualitative ones.

4   Performance Management and Staff Appraisal: Myth and Reality

This section analyses the data received through the two questionnaires for staff and managers, Appendices A and B, unstructured interviews in order to seek clarifications, following the analysis of the collected data from the questionnaires, observations, reports as well as government/official and banking documents. The questionnaire was distributed to the banks in Muscat and their branches in other regions, according to availability: Dhofar, Al Batinah, Al Dakhelia and Al Dhahera. Though a request was made to all respondents to reply, there were *720* which were received. Out of these 720 subjects *577* answered the questionnaires completely: *441* were employers below managerial cadre (subordinates) and *136* were managers of various capacities. In other words, 80.14% of all subjects responded well to the questionnaires, by answering all the applicable required sections. The others were ruled out to avoid any bias.

4.1   Age of Respondents

Table 4.1 illustrates the data collected about the age of the respondents.
- The peak age group for the managers occurs at 50-59 years, where as for sub-ordinates it is 30-39. It means that the managers are older than the sub-ordinates.
- The managers are almost two decades older than their sub-ordinates in general.
- More than 44% of the subordinates are in the 30-39 years age group, while 41.1% of the managers are in the 50-59 years age group.

Table 4.1: Age Distribution of Managers and Non-Managers of Actual Respondents

Category		20-29 Years	30-39 Years	40-49 Years	50-59 Years	> 59 Years	Total
Managers	No.	12	19	45	56	4	136
	%	8.8%	14.0%	33.1%	41.1%	2.9%	100%
Subordinates	No..	45	197	178	16	6	441
	%	10.2%	44.6%	40.3%	3.5%	1.4%	100%

4.2   Gender Distribution

The collected data illustrates the gender distribution, Table 4.2. We can draw following conclusions from this gender related data:

- Females subordinates are more frequently found than male subordinates
- Male managers/seniors are more than female managers.

Table 4.2: Gender Distribution Managers and Non-Managers of Actual Respondents

	Managers		Sub-ordinates		Total
Category	Male	Female	Male	Female	
Number	94	42	201	240	577
%	69.1	30.9	45.6	54.4	100/100

4.3   Qualifications and Level of Training

Table 4.3 and Figure 4.1 summarise the qualifications of the subject who took part in the study. It is obvious that the managers are more academically qualified, with undergraduate and postgraduate qualifications.

Table 4.3: Qualifications of Managers and Non-Managers of Actual Respondents

Category		BA	PG/PG Diploma	BBA in Banking or Similar	Dip. in Banking	Other Qualifications	Total
Managers	No.	32	18	7	65	14	**136**
	%	**23.53%**	**13.23%**	**5.15%**	**47.79%**	**10.29%**	**100%**
Subordinates	No.	74	2	47	308	10	**441**
	%	16.8%	0.45%	10.66%	69.9%	2.3%	**100%**

Figure 4.1: Qualifications of Managers and Non-Managers

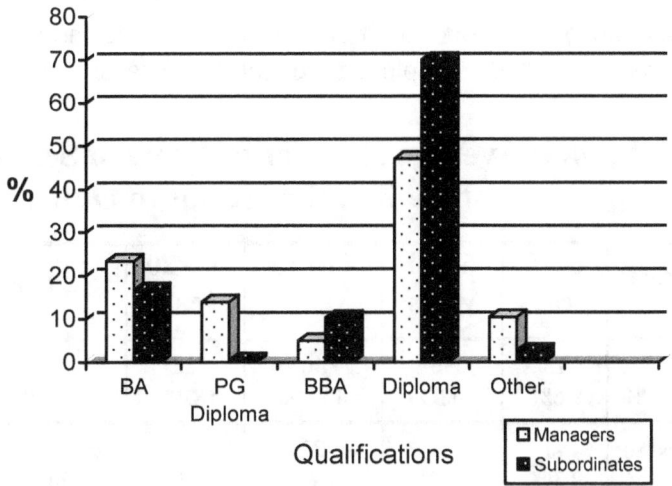

The data give the following information:

- There is a large percentage of managers with diploma qualifications.
- The diploma is also a qualification which is held by many subordinates.
- There is a visible trend in this sector that there are more senior/managerial staff who have the minimum/other qualifications compared to junior staff.

- When we look at the difference between managers and subordinates, there is a positive difference among bachelor degree holders, PG/PG diploma holders. But there is a negative difference (i.e. manager with less qualification than subordinates) exists among BBA and diploma holders.

This can be related to the fact the senior members joined the banking sector at the early stage of the renaissance era, when the number of schools and clinics, not hospitals, count be counted on one hand. But now, education and health care services are available all over the country. So, it is natural to find the young Omani are more qualified or trained than the earlier generations.

4.4   Years of Service in the Banking Industry

Table 4.4 shows the work experience in the banking industry, as the randomly selected study sample may reflect the actual situation.

Table 4.4: Average Number of Years of Service in the Banking Sector in Oman

Experience/ Position	0 – 5 years	6– 10 years	11– 15 years	16- 20 years	> 20 years	Total
Managers No.	13	36	46	25	16	**136**
%	9.6%	26.5%	33.8%	18.4%	11.8%	**100%**
Subordinates No.	41	34	72	55	239	**441**
%	9.3%	7.7%	16.3%	12.5%	54.2%	**100%**

Figure 4.2 also shows the distribution of years of experience across managers and their subordinates.

**Figure 4.2: Average Number of Years of Service
in the Banking Sector in Oman**

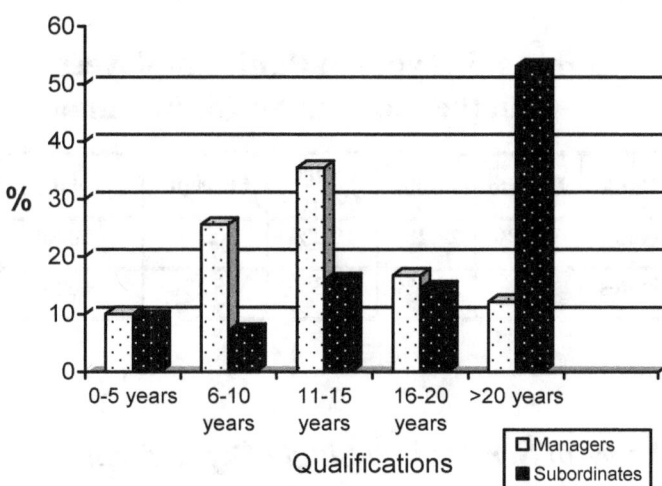

The following points are evident from Figure 4.4. :

- The largest group of managers fall into the 11-15 years of experience category, where as there are more subordinates fall into the 20 years one.
- It appears that the most of the bank staff become managers around their 10th year of experience. If they do not become, due to lower qualification, they remain in the bank as subordinates.

4.5   Classification of the Different Types of Bank Employees

Table 4.5 illustrates the distribution/percentages of managers and subordinates according to the type of bank in the sector. This can be summed up as follows.

- There are more managers in foreign banks who responded to the survey than in any other type of bank.
- The greatest number of subordinates are in public as well as public central bank.

- Based on the survey results and observations, it appears that all the subordinates are quickly promoted as managers in foreign banks than other types.

Table 4.5: Types of Bank Employees in the Banking Sector in Oman

Type of Bank	Private	Public	Public-Central	Foreign	Specialised	Total
Managers	18.3%	28.2%	19.2%	30.3%	4.0%	100%
Subordinates	7.9%	39.0%	29.3%	15.2%	8.6%	100%

4.6   Years of Service in a Single Department

Table 4.5 indicates the data collected (in %) from the questionnaires indicating the length of service in a single department. Accordingly, the following conclusions can be drawn:

- Managers do not stay in single department more than one or two years. There are very few managers who stay in a department after 5 years.
- On the contrary, subordinates seem to remain in the same department for a long time.   One wonders, if the subordinates have a choice or they are told by the management to stay ther.

Table 4.6: Average Years of Service in of Managers and Subordinates a Single Department in the Banking Sector in Oman

Years of Stay in the Same Department	0 - 12 Months	1-2 years	2 - 3 years	3 - 4 years	>4 years	Total
Managers	20.7%	39.1%	20.1%	12.2%	7.9%	100%
Subordinates	21.9%	14.4%	6.2%	4.4%	53.1%	100%

4.7 Perception of Staff Development, Knowledge and Skills and the Appraisal Process

Responses to the subordinates' questionnaire, Appendix A, were analysed to identify the perception of the subordinates of their knowledge and skills for the implementation of the goals and objectives of the organisation, Table 4.7.

Table 4.7: Level of Knowledge and Skills of Subordinates in the Banking Sector in Oman

Parameter		1*	2*	3*	4*	5*	Total	Mode	Median	Mean	S.D.	D.F.	Level of Sign.
Planning of bank everyday activities	N	12	3	48	285	93	441	4	4	4.0	0.94	4	P>0.05
	%	2.8	0.7	11.1	64.6	20.8	100						
Implementing plans	N	9	9	81	252	90	441	4	4	3.92	0.99	4	P<0.05
	%	2.1	2.1	18.4	57.1	20.4	100						
Assessment of customer requirements	N	3	3	57	219	162	441	4	4	4.23	0.91	4	P>0.25
	%	0.7	0.7	12.2	49.7	36.6	100						
Implementing of banking performance standards	N	3	9	96	243	90	441	4	4	3.92	0.96	4	P<0.20
	%	0.7	2.1	22	55.3	20.6	100						
Knowledge in accounts/ finance current affairs	N	9	15	45	225	147	441	4	4	4.1	0.91	4	P>0.05
	%	2.1	3.4	10.3	51	33.1	100						
Banking competencies	N	0	9	87	237	108	441	4	4	4.0	0.91	4	P<0.05
	%	0	2.1	20	53.8	24.8	100						
Interpersonal relations	N	6	6	81	240	108	441	4	4	4.0	0.74	4	P>0.05
	%	1.4	1.4	18.3	54.2	24.6	100						
customer counselling skills	N	15	15	138	201	72	441	4	4	3.7	0.97	4	P>0.25
	%	3.5	3.5	31.3	45.8	16	100						

* 1 = Very Poor, 2 = Poor,; 3 = Average; Good; 4 = Very Good; 5 = Excellent

The majority of the respondents perceived themselves as having a high level of knowledge and skills. They are satisfactory in the different areas including accounts/finance current affairs, banking competencies and customer care, being able to meet customers' requirements. On the other hand, most of these subordinates do not have the needed qualifications or experience in the banking sector except being introduced by a colleague of the same background and qualification when joining the bank. In fact, most of the banks require new staff to go through an orientation programme when joining the bank. However, such a theoretical programme, in most cases/banks, is not taken seriously by all parties. Responses to the interviews and observations revealed many issues. One of them is that this could be due to the fact it is perceived as just a quality assurance requirement, in addition to following the requirements of the Ministry of Manpower. This is because the ministry require all private sector organisations to train Omani school leavers to be employable. Actually, many of the young the Omani employees indicated that such orientation programmes are usually not beneficial, as they are perceived as a formality to be theoretically qualified for the new job. They also felt that those who trained them are not competent and they also perceive such a programme as a formality.

Table 4.8: Method of Performance Appraisal

Question	Responses No.	Responses %
• A formal system of regular appraisals with reviews of past performance, setting of objectives	72	16.33%
• Informal, but regular reviews involving discussions about past performance and agreed actions for the future.	99	22.45%
• Informal, *ad hoc* reviews, undertaken especially when there is a performance problem	176	39.91%
• Not reviewed	80	18.14%
• No response	14	3.17&

In the same section through open-ended questions, when asking subordinates about which skill(s) is difficult to learn or inculcate, they responded that customer counselling is a very difficult skill to acquire. They also perceived the supervision of the trainees as a demanding or high level skill. It is indeed important that performance of every employee should be measured adequately in the organisation. Tables 4.8 and 4.9 summarise the data collected on this aspect and the evaluation of the process of the staff/subordinates' appraisal and its implications on training, promotion, demotion, or not referred to at all.

Table 4.8 shows that a 360-degree staff evaluation and good practice are hardly being taken seriously by the management and staff, in most banks: national or local and international ones. This is in spite of the fact that most of the managers in these banks emphasised the importance of implementing a 360-degree staff evaluation and good practice in their banks. However, during the interviews many of the managers including the HR managers indicated they do not have the time to do so as it is theoretically required. On the other hand, the needed forms are usually completed, as needed evidence. Actually, the responses of the subordinates do not contradict their managers' implantation of the evaluation process. Briefly, evaluation is done in a traditional manner, but the routine filling of particular forms gives it the needed modern touch.

Interviews with managers and subordinates revealed that the actual appraisal evaluation does not usually result in guiding the managers to identify the weaknesses or strengths of the staff, but it is used to justify the renewing of the staff contracts and giving increments to the ones the managers or supervisors decided to be granted. If fact, some of the managers including Omani HR managers complained that the Omani labour law makes it semi-impossible to terminate the employment of an Omani, even if he/she will be replaced by another national. So, managers and subordinates are actually in agreement that staff appraisal does not usually help in identifying those who should be trained, promoted or demoted. On the other hand, staff training and promotion seem to be done in the traditional way, according to the perception of the manager of his chosen staff.

Table 4.9: Utilisation of Performance Appraisal

• Training	14.2
• Promotion	17.8
• Demotion	2.6
• Rotation	9.6
• Not used	52.3
• No response	3.5

Accordingly, the first null hypothesis is accepted.

H. 1	"Staff performance identified through appraisal process cannot be described as a 360-degree evaluation which is transparent and helps to identify the weaknesses and strengths of the staff in order to provide the needed training or award incentives or promotion."	Accepted

4.8 Staff Perception of the Feedback Process Following their Appraisal

Table 4.10 below illustrates the responses to the subordinates' questionnaire, Appendix A. Actually, the responses of most of the staff to the items related to the feedback process following the appraisal tended to be negative indicating that the actual appraisal process does not meet its set goals and objectives. It is also not conducted throughout the year. Furthermore, not all subordinates are evaluated and consequently no feedback is provided. However, some staff members still feel that their managers inspire them to do their best. On the other hand, the subordinates contradict that in other situations. In addition, responses to the questionnaire and during the semi-structured interviews reflected a feeling of frustration as they are not given the opportunity to make comments in general and on the result of their performance. That can be explained according to Hofstede's (1983) classification according to national cultures, as most of the managers are either Indians or Omanis.

Table 4.10: Staff Perception of the Feedback Process Following their Appraisal

Parameter		1*	2*	3*	4*	5*	Total	Mode	Median	Mean	S.D.	D.F.	Level of Sign.
Objectives to be achieved are known by individuals to be assessed	N	140	132	93	61	15	441	2	2	2.13	0.1	4	P>0.05
	%	31.7	30.0	21.1	13.8	3.4	100						
Performance standards expected from staff are clear and understood by all	N	63	81	120	117	63	441	3	3	3.10	0.7	4	P>0.20
	%	14	18.2	27.3	26.6	14	100						
Constructive feedback on performance appraisal results is provided on a regular basis	N	214	185	17	35	17	441	1	1	1.98	0.11	4	P<0.25
	%	48.4	41.9	3.9	7.9	3.9	100						
Feedback of how staff is performing is provided throughout the year	N	140	132	93	61	15	441	2	2	2.13	0.1	4	P>0.05
	%	31.7	30.0	21.1	13.8	3.4	100						
Prompt action is taken when performance falls below acceptable standards	N	63	81	120	117	63	441	3	3	3.10	0.7	4	P>0.20
	%	14	18.2	27.3	26.6	14	100						
My managers/supervisor inspires me to do my best	N	140	132	93	61	15	441	2	2	2.13	0.1	4	P>0.05
	%	31.7	30.0	21.1	13.8	3.4	100						
Staff are given opportunity to make comments on the results of their performance	N	214	185	17	35	17	441	1	1	1.98	0.11	4	P<0.25
	%	48.4	41.9	3.9	7.9	3.9	100						

* 1 = Strongly Disagree, 2 = Disagree,; 3 = Uncertain; 4 = Agree; 5 = Strongly Agree

Table 4.11: Remuneration, Benefits and Recognition as Perceived by Subordinates

Parameter		1*	2*	3*	4*	5*	Total	Mode	Median	Mean	S.D.	D.F.	Level of Sign.
Your remuneration is competitive compared to other similar organisations.	N	138	102	117	75	9	441	1	2.3	2.4	0.11	4	P<0.05
		31.3	23.4	26.2	17.0	2.1	100						
Remuneration is in accordance with your experience.	N	144	75	91	113	18	441	1	2.7	2.5	0.11	4	P>0.01
	%	32.7	17.0	20.6	25.6	4.1	100						
Remuneration is in accordance with your job responsibility	N	123	108	81	114	15	441	1	2	2.5	0.10	4	P<0.10
	%	27.9	24.5	18.2	25.9	3.5	100						
Fringe benefits are known to you	N	99	54	117	141	30	441	4	3	2.9	0.10	4	P<0.25
	%	22.4	12.3	26.5	32.0	6.8	100						
You are satisfied with your fringe benefits.	N	138	102	117	75	9	441	1	3	2.4	0.11	4	P<0.05
	%	31.3	23.1	26.5	17.0	2.1	100						
Opportunities exist for career advancement.	N	109	102	113	90	27	441	3	3	2.6	0.08	4	P>0.05
	%	24.7	23.1	25.7	20.4	6.1	100						
Hardworking are recognised.	N	213	123	63	24	18	441	1	2	1.9	0.18	4	P<0.05
	%	48.3	27.9	14.3	5.4	4.1	100						

* 1 = Strongly Disagree, 2 = Disagree,; 3 = Uncertain; 4 = Agree; 5 = Strongly Agree

Table 4.11 reflects the negative perception of the subordinates in national and international banks as they perceived remunerations, benefits and even recognition are not awarded as a result of staff appraisal, competence, responsibilities and hard work. So, what is the value of staff appraisal?

Table 4.12: Management Style as Perceived by Subordinates

Parameter		1*	2*	3*	4*	5*	Total	Mode	Median	Mean	S.D.	D.F.	Level of Sign.
My manager/ supervisor inspires me to do my best.	N	72	39	196	86	48	**441**	**3**	**3**	**3.22**	0.13	4	P<0.05
	%	16.3	8.8	44.4	19.5	10.9	**100**						
Judgement about my performance is fair.	N	60	90	129	141	21	**441**	**3**	**3**	**2.94**	0.11	4	P>0.02
	%	13.6	20.4	29.3	32	4.8	**100**						
This organisation's mission is understood by everyone who works here	N	42	57	168	156	18	**441**	**3**	**3**	**3.12**	0.16	4	P<0.25
	%	9.5	12.9	38.1	35.4	4.1	**100**						
The people I work with are comfortable in suggesting changes and improvements to each other.	N	69	93	138	114	27	**441**	**3**	**3**	**2.85**	0.1	4	P<0.25
	%	15.6	21.1	31.3	25.9	6.1	**100**						
Senior managers in this organisation are open to new ideas and suggestions.	N	96	150	72	90	33	**441**	**2**	**2**	**2.57**	0.1	4	P<0.05
	%	21.8	34	16.3	20.4	7.5	**100**						
I am clear about the objectives I need to achieve.	N	81	114	123	117	18	**441**	**3**	**3**	**2.80**	0.1	4	P>0.01
	%	18.4	23.1	27.9	26.5	4.1	**100**						
I trust and respect my immediate supervisor.	N	9	23	192	156	61	**441**	**3**	**3**	**3.54**	0.25	4	P<0.01
	%	2.1	5.2	43.5	35.4	13.8	**100**						

* 1 = Strongly Disagree, 2 = Disagree,; 3 = Uncertain; 4 = Agree; 5 = Strongly Agree

Responses to Table 4.12 are mostly inconclusive, as the mode and the median of most responses are '3', which means 'uncertain', but mostly in disagreement. One may wonder is it because of the respondents' cultural backgrounds which are explained by Hofstede as the subordinates were asked to evaluate their superiors/managers. Or are the subordinates not satisfied with the appraisal process? Or it is a combination of the two options combined.

Accordingly, the second null hypothesis is partly accepted.

H. 1	"Human resources management factors, including staff appraisal feedback; leadership and management, as well as knowledge and skills of managers do not affect the performance of bank employees, their remunerations, benefits and recognition."	Partly accepted

4.9 Managers' Responses

Table 4.13 summarises the data obtained from the questionnaire on various aspects.

Table 4.13: Management Functions

Factors	No %	Yes %	Total %
Providing training to employees	21.4	78.6	100
One-to-one performance interview related to performance outcome	61.1	38.9	100
Placement of staff according to skills	26.2	73.8	100
Orientation of new staff	9.5	90.5	100
Managing conflict	16.7	83.3	100
Operational research	52.4	47.6	100
Counselling of employees	31.0	69.0	100

- These results indicate that the majority of the managers believe that orientation of new staff is one of the important management function. At the same time they consider that performance interview is **not** an important management function.

- They further confirmed that managing conflict is as one of the difficult management function that they handle. Next to that was operations research which seems difficult for them.

Table 4.14: Managers Knowledge and Skills

Parameter		1*	2*	3*	4*	5*	Total	Mode	Median	Mean	S.D.	D.F.	Level of Sign.
Banking service policy implementation	N	0	4	66	62	4	136	3	3	3.48	0.22	4	P>0.05
	%	0	2.9	48.6	45.6	2.9	100						
Planning service delivery	N	0	15	55	58	8	136	3	3	3.32	0.16	4	P<0.25
	%	0	11.0	40.4	42.6	6.0	100						
Audit	N	11	11	55	58	1	136	4	3	3.20	0.13	4	P<0.02
	%	8.1	8.1	40.4	42.6	0.8	100						
Development of banking performance standards	N	14	20	66	32	4	136	3	3	3.18	0.17	4	P<0.05
	%	10.3	14.7	48.5	23.5	3	100						
Development of competencies	N	11	11	70	35	9	136	3	3	3.15	0.21	4	P<0.20
	%	8.1	8.1	51.5	25.7	6.6	100						
Skills development	N	6	16	44	55	15	136	4	4	3.42	0.19	4	P>0.20
	%	4.4	11.8	32.4	40.4	11.0	100						
Interpersonal relations	N	4	16	22	70	24	441	4	4	3.69	0.21	4	P>0.20
	%	3.0	11.8	16.2	51.5	17.5	136						
Counselling skills	N	11	16	55	46	8	441	3	3	3.10	0.20	4	P>0.05
	%	8.1	11.8	40.4	33.7	6.0	136						

* 1 = Strongly Disagree, 2 = Disagree; 3 = Uncertain; 4 = Strongly Agree; 5 = Strongly Agree

Table 4.15: Management and Leadership Style

Parameter		1*	2*	3*	4*	Total	Mode	Median	Mean	S.D.	D.F.	Level of Sign.
Leadership style is the way in which the management philosophy manifests itself in practice	N	22	12	41	61	136	4	3	3.04	0.14	3	P>0.05
	%	16.2	8.8	30.1	44.9	100						
The leadership style over the last 20 years has been one of democratic leadership	N	17	57	45	17	136	2	2.4	2.46	0.15	3	P<0.20
	%	12.5	42.0	33.0	12.5	100						
Problem solving is more successful when managed immediately by the supervisor, rather than involving the specific subordinates	N	2	63	36	33	136	2	3	2.71	0.19	3	P>0.05
	%	1.5	46.4	24.7	24.4	100						
Managers should possess adequate communication skills	N	0	3	38	95	136	4	4	3.31	0.39	3	P<0.05
	%	0.0	2.2	28.0	69.8	100						
Due to the heavy work load of managers, it is not expected that they should have a training function	N	2	63	36	33	136	2	3	2.32	0.19	3	P>0.05
	%	1.5	46.4	24.7	24.4	100						
Customer care is the primary function of the manager; therefore personnel management can be managed by the personnel department	N	28	48	15	45	136	2	2	2.57	0.14	3	P<0.02
	%	20.6	35.3	11.0	33.1	100						

* 1 = Don't know, 2 = Don't agree; 3 = Tend to agree; 4 = Fully agree

Tables 4.14 and 4.15 summarises the data obtained from managers on the knowledge and skills aspect as well as their perceptions of management and leadership style. Briefly, managers have scored interpersonal relations as their best skills. The least that they possess was banking performance standards. On the other hand, the majority of the subordinates were not sure about the development competencies of their managers.

Table 4.16: Performance Appraisal

Parameter	Response (%)
A formal system of regular appraisals with reviews of past performance, setting of objectives	22.1
Informal, but regular reviews involving discussions about past performance and agreed actions for the future	2.9
Informal, *ad hoc* reviews, undertaken especially when there is a performance problem	33.4
Not reviewed	41.6
No response	4.8

Table 4.16 shows the managers' views on the performance review system. Although performance reviews were not conducted often, it was done on an *ad hoc* basis indicating a problem in this area.

Management and Leadership

Table 4.17 indicates the manager's score on management and leadership. Findings indicate that motivation is perceived as a very important factor for the employees to work with. At the same time, managers do not accept that their style is an autocratic type of management.

Table 4.17: Management and Leadership

Parameter		1*	2*	3*	4*	Total	Mode	Median	Mean	S.D.	D.F.	Level of Sign.
Extrinsic motivation of employees involves stimulation of goal achievement.	N	15	9	46	66	**136**						
	%	11.0	6.6	33.8	48.5	**100**	4	3	3.20	0.2	3	P>0.02
Management's leadership style has an effect on the level of performance inclination.	N	16	15	39	66	**136**						
	%	11.8	11	28.7	48.5	**100**	4	3	3.14	0.21	3	P>0.25
A position of authority is required in management positions to ensure successful influencing of subordinates.	N	10	6	58	62	**136**						
	%	7.4	4.4	42.6	45.6	**100**	3	3	3.26	0.26	3	P<0.25
Traditionally, managers in Oman have had an autocratic style of management.	N	18	33	58	27	**136**						
	%	13.1	17.5	42.5	19.9	**100**	3	3	2.69	0.1	3	P>0.05
Participative management involves shared decision-making.	N	3	12	34	87	**136**						
	%	2.2	8.8	25	64	**100**	3	3	3.51	0.31	3	P>0.05
Employees, who receive frequent feedback concerning their performance, are usually more highly motivated than those who do not.	N	10	9	15	102	**136**						
	%	7.4	6.6	11.0	75	**100**	4	4	3.54	0.37	3	P<0.05

* 1 = Don't know, 2 = Don't agree; 3 = Tend to agree; 4 = Fully agree

4.10 *Conclusion*

The findings revealed by the different test instruments directly imply that there is cause to be greatly concerned about the current scenario of HRM in banks of Oman. As illustrated in the literature review, the workforce cannot perform better if they are non-responsive and inefficient. This in turn affects quality issues at banks. The literature indicates that there are some actions and ways to achieve the expected outcomes. Those actions include improving working conditions, improving motivation and productivity of the workforce. It was also established that in-service trainings on management skills with better remuneration and incentives will enable these changes in banks.

The very first fact that was revealed from the study is in the area of 'knowledge and skills'. Only 30% of the respondents felt that they have the 'adequate' knowledge and skills. The remaining 70% which is big enough illustrates that there is a need for training on increasing quality in the workplace. As discussed in literature while addressing the issues of HRM at service sectors, customers will categorically point out quality issues delivered by the bank staff. So it is important that each employee is clearly aware about how to recognise quality. Without this it is almost difficult to inculcate quality. Quality thus cannot be delivered without providing adequate trainings on knowledge and skills.

Banks in Oman are introducing new products/services through their branches due to globalisation pressure. Before introducing them it is imperative to 'teach' every employee about the new product/service. Generally, managers receive many complaints from customers. Out of these one of the main complaints which occur frequently is 'I don't know about this, please contact that person...' To stop this management should introduce any new product to its employees first before introducing it to the customers. This will in-turn increases the confidence of the staff and will keep them better informed. Every customer will receive updates and the latest service from the branch.

The next issue to 'knowledge and skills' is performance appraisal and utilisation. The questionnaire unilaterally revealed that this issue is not handled appropriately by the bank management. Even after-appraisal scenarios in banks were not observed as conducive. There is no mentoring at all. Mentoring, undoubtedly, is a great tool to enhance performance which is in accordance with Grote's (2002) observation. As the employees are not satisfied with performance appraisal nor with its consequences. In other words, the very aim of performance appraisal system is to be questioned. De-motivated or under-motivated employees will not perform well and consequently will position the branch under performed. There is no place for quality during this underperformance and the competitive advantage of bank which is achieved through its sustainable service will be permanently affected.

Remuneration, rewards and recognition which is an exercise closely related to the performance appraisal issue is again poorly managed in banks. Bank staff is not happy when they compare their salaries with other banks or allied industries. Only below 27% of subordinates were satisfied with the existing salary structure. Sharpley (2002) and Nickols (2003) illustrated that this is one of the very important factors which will decide the degree of motivation among staff. As long as this issue is not taken care seriously the underperformance of the employees cannot be altered even all the other issues are addressed appropriately. Therefore the findings of this study reiterate the importance of monetary benefits on delivering better performance and producing a performing workforce.

Finally, the leadership and management issue is identified as a positive factor affecting the performance of bank staff. It was found that more than 80% of staff trusts their bosses/supervisors. At the same time, as demanded by around 40% of staff, if the superiors consult their subordinates this factor can contribute to better performance. The questionnaire also revealed that knowledge and skills of managers greatly influence the knowledge and skills of subordinates. So, the management should ensure that leadership is created in such a way that knowledge and skills are balanced on two sides, i.e., leadership and followers' side.

Consequently, the study questions, 4.2, are answered with particular reference to banks in Oman and consequently the Omani economy. Therefore, the study null hypothesis, 4.3, is partly rejected:

H1.	Human resources management factors including knowledge and skills; performance appraisal and utilisation; remuneration; rewards and recognition; leadership and management; as well as knowledge and skills of managers do *not* affect the performance of bank employees in Oman.	Partly Rejected

In the light of these findings and conclusions, there are a few recommendations which will enable better performance from workforce not only in banks in Oman but also in other parts of the world too, including developing and developed countries. The following chapter concludes the study with some recommendations.

5 Conclusion and Recommendations

5.1 Key Points

This chapter illustrates the conclusions that can be made from the data analysis of this project and also recommendations for improvement of effectiveness of the employees in banks.

The entire study was based on the fact that every country's economic system, including the Sultanate of Oman, depends on banking and the bank's performance in turn depends on the performance of the employees. As there are noted problems in the bank's HRM, this study provided empirical evidence for the factors affecting performance of a bank employee.

As the reviewed literature substantiated the room for improvement and ways to improve, the data reflected that both banks and government have much to do on these aspects. As it is seen in the background study banking sector provides employment for the youth, their performance at the bank highly affects the HR pool of the nation. The study revealed both positive as well as negative factors that affect the performance of a banker.

This study had the specific objective of determining the factors affecting performance, and identifying the skills and knowledge that managers should possess to supervise their subordinates in an optimal way. After comparing the collected data and the literature review a series of recommendations is proposed.

In the literature review, a synthesised model of HRM viz. performance model was made in accordance with the framework by Sharpley (2002). It was modelled on perception, motivation and performance practices that influence bank workers.

The very first aim of the study was to identify the factors affecting the performance of bank workers. The presented data showed both positive as well as negative factors affecting the performance of workers. As the positive factors are motivating further and negative factors are de-motivators it is important to analyse both of them.

The following conclusions were made from the study:

1. Knowledge and skills

Almost one third of bank employees considered that they have necessary and sufficient skills in conducting the every day business of bank. They also revealed that they need to acquire the skills to improve quality care. As the banking industry is becoming more competitive, maintaining quality is an important issue. Therefore it has to be seriously taken into consideration by managerial personnel.

Nearly one third of the respondents exhibited that they possess skills to facilitate in-service training and self assessments. But their concern was delivering quality service. Most of them were not aware of the bank's policy of quality and their idea regarding quality in service. As Oman has a heterogeneous population with expatriates and locals, knowledge of English also leads to better customer care, as admitted by many respondents.

2. Performance appraisal and utilisation:

The present study clearly revealed that the procedure for conducting the same is not what is to be expected. The collected data enables us to conclude that there is no feedback mechanism to develop the employees further in the next year. They also indicated that the procedure does not allow them to record their comment and suggestions for a better procedure and outcome. This became evident as staff need mentoring and may be further training. As Dick Grote (2002) points out, only mentoring will enhance the performance.

The importance of this factor is not taken seriously by the banks' management. All the respondents stated that this is done on an ad hoc basis. They uniformly complained that appraisals were not aimed at identifying skill gaps or performance. As the method of measurement is very poor, the control over the staff will also be evidently poor. This is emphasised by most of the study sample, e.g., there is no place for individual comments or self-appraisal in all the banks. Therefore, bank personnel do not get any kind of feedback to improve further in consecutive years. This raises a question: What is the value of staff appraisal if it does not result in staff guidance, development and further training leading to a better quality of banking customer service?

3. Remuneration, rewards and recognition:

More than half of the respondents (both managers and subordinates) were not satisfied about their salary. They complained that it is not comparable with other industries/sectors. Briefly, 27% of the respondents believed that bank salaries are better than the salaries given by other sectors, while one-third of the study sample described the banks' salaries as being 'not poor.' This proves that this factor positively affects their performance. At the same time, another factor pointed out by the respondents was staff expectation of increment for earning additional qualifications. This goes in line with Sharpley (2002) who emphasised that it is individual perception of anticipation of success, praise and recognition which is consequently associated with high performance. It is also supported by Nickols (2003) who indicated that these factors are motivating factors which we recommend to be taken seriously by employers and managers not only in the banking sector, but also in other sectors. In so doing, better performance, higher quality of services and a higher and efficient productivity will be a natural outcome.

The respondents stated that satisfaction and having a sense of achievement are important to find their work rewarding. But more than 50% of the respondents indicated that they get used to receiving poor acknowledgement and recognition, if any, as a reward for better job delivery. This shows that this factor affects their performance positively. Naturally, the more deserved acknowledgement and recognition the staff receive, the better the performance of the bank staff, and others in different service and production sectors.

4. Leadership and management

This study also revealed that performance levels of the workers are highly affected by the leadership and management. More than 80% of managers as well as subordinates indicated that they trust their immediate supervisors. But at the same time, around 40% of subordinates felt that they are consulted by their bosses.

Thus, the leadership of the supervisors not only affects the organisation, but also it affects their subordinates in the way how they manage the different departments and the organisation as a whole. Indeed, the leadership style influences the subordinates in delivering better services to customers in synchronous with the organisational quality policy. Once this happens, then the performance of the individual staff will be enhanced automatically, as a natural outcome due to staff loyalty and commitment to the organisation.

5. Knowledge and skills of managers

The knowledge and skills of their managers were also assessed by the respondents. Their evaluation of their managers and supervisors ranged from 'good' to 'average.' A very important outcome was that one-third of subjects felt that their supervisors possessed only average knowledge and skills. They also indicated that they were not happy over how banking standards were maintained and how performance appraisals were administered.

This perhaps is one of the distressing outcomes of this study. It is thus concluded that some managers do not possess the skills to plan and supervise the implementation of banking services. They are not even capable of supporting and guiding their subordinates to implement better servicing in their branches.

Furthermore, during the semi-structured interviews, most staff members, managers and subordinates emphasised the fact that staff appraisals are conducted in a way to theoretically follow bank procedures and to look transparent. But in reality, managers and supervisors follow the old, traditional and hierarchal approach to meet the deadline of this uncomfortable process for all parties. Furthermore, there was a general agreement, the overall appraisal is decided first, and then the details are adjusted. This was also described as a subjective process in most cases.

Briefly, the study explored the factors affecting the performance of bank staff. The above-mentioned findings and issues need to be immediately addressed to ensure sustainable progress in this dynamic banking business environment. A framework with the broad areas comprising the factors is to be developed by each bank and its branches while being consistent with the quality policy. Such a framework may include activities like advocacy, increasing the knowledge and expertise of the workforce; development of leadership and management skills; better performance management and a feedback system with continuing professional development.

5.2   Conclusion and Recommendations

Based on these findings, the following recommendations are made to capitalise the positive factors and minimise the negative factors that affect the performance of an employee in banks.

1. Enhancement and development of the banking profession

This can be realised using different approaches. Launching an awareness programme to lure talented students directly from colleges is one of the effective ways. Advertisements and campaigns to attract more talented youth to this profession will increase the overall performance of the human resources pool for banking. Various scholarly bodies, universities and bank managements can sit together to sort out special courses for the present day's requirement. Therefore, cooperation between the banking sector and the training institutes, e.g., Sultan Qaboos University, the Higher Colleges of Technology and the Banking Institute academic boards is a necessity to ensure that their product meets the actual needs of the banking industry. In fact, these training institutes urge the cooperation of the business and industrial sectors by having representatives of these sectors on their academic boards. But, in reality, it was reported by officials of these institutes that representatives of the business industry are too busy to be actively involved in developing the training programmes of such training institutes.

2. Developing knowledge and expertise

Continuous professional development programmes and effective in-service programmes will enable high performance. The identified skills gap through appraisals should be practically reflected on the short training courses for both managers and subordinates. In other words, the purpose of the appraisal process should not be limited to just debarring the employees from an increment.

3. Enhancing performance management system

It is very clear that the present appraisal system does not provide the expected feedback. Therefore, a radical change is required on this aspect. New standards should be defined and management should help the staff to meet the standards through various awareness and training programmes.

4. Motivation

As the study revealed, the problem in motivation is that the bank management should motivate employers through remuneration and benefits at the same level of other industries. This will result in improving the level of satisfaction and staff performance. Therefore, managers should be creative in finding ways to motivate employees.

5. Pay structure and leadership

In addition to these, an overall review of the pay structure, and the arrangement of leadership and executive development programmes will enhance the performance of the banking staff as well as others.

6. **Mentoring and guidance**

The importance of mentoring is also another important issue particularly for new staff. This is needed as most of the Omani staff are school leavers with no experience in the world of work. Therefore, a supervision mechanism with proper feedback will improve job performance, job satisfaction and provide motivation. This should naturally result in better quality of work, better quality of service provided to customers and pride in one's job leading to loyalty and commitment to the bank/organisation. This will also decrease the number of the staff leaving the bank after investing in their recruitment and training.

This study therefore indicates that now is the time for an overall restructuring of the HR system in the banking sector in Oman. By doing so, not only the quality of the banks' human resources will develop and become more efficient, but also the performance of the banks, which consequently affects the economy of Oman positively. In so doing, the successful banks would be the ones able to use their human resources as the unique competitive edge which is difficult to clone or copy by competitors.

Therefore, the study recommends to those banks as well as to other organisations to identify the most important aspects of performance management (PM) and to explore good practices models and implementation. In so doing, adopting the performance management systems (PMS), and the performance management good practice (PMGP) model should be the starting point.

6 The Implementation of Performance Management Good Practice Model in Omani Banks

6.1 Introduction

Taking into consideration the study findings and its recommendations, this chapter aims at proposing the performance management good practice (PMGP) model to help to develop the appraisal system in Omani banks as well as other organisations. This should lead to improving the employees' level of work efficiency and a low percentage of staff turnover, which is also a natural outcome of staff satisfaction, loyalty and commitment to the bank or the organisation.

Indeed, local and global business environment is changing rapidly. Profit (banks, business and industrial companies) and non-profit organisations (charities and government organisations) have to develop performance management systems (PMS) in order to achieve a competitive edge (Barney, 1986 and 1991; Torrington, 2005). The function of managers and supervisors is to manage organisational performance, i.e. to manage all aspects related to the setting and achievement of organisational goals and strategy. In other words, managers need to establish expectations, in collaboration with their employees and stakeholders, agree upon ways to measure performance relative to those expectations, measure or assess performance overtime, and use those measures to provide feedback and take action (McNamara, 2006).

So, performance management (PM) can be described as a systematic process for improving organisational performance by developing the performance of individuals and teams (Armstrong, 2006; Bratton and Gold, 2003; Kelliny, 2010). This is to achieve a high level of efficiency in a turbulent business environment. This is usually caused by changing employment legislation, changing workforce composition. Furthermore, it is the norm in many banks in Oman to see managers and heads of departments are being challenged to utilise their staff more efficiently. This is to ensure gaining a competitive edge over other competitive local and international banks and other business organisations in Oman and the Gulf region.

Performance Management Systems (PMS)

Figure 6.1: Performance Management Cycle

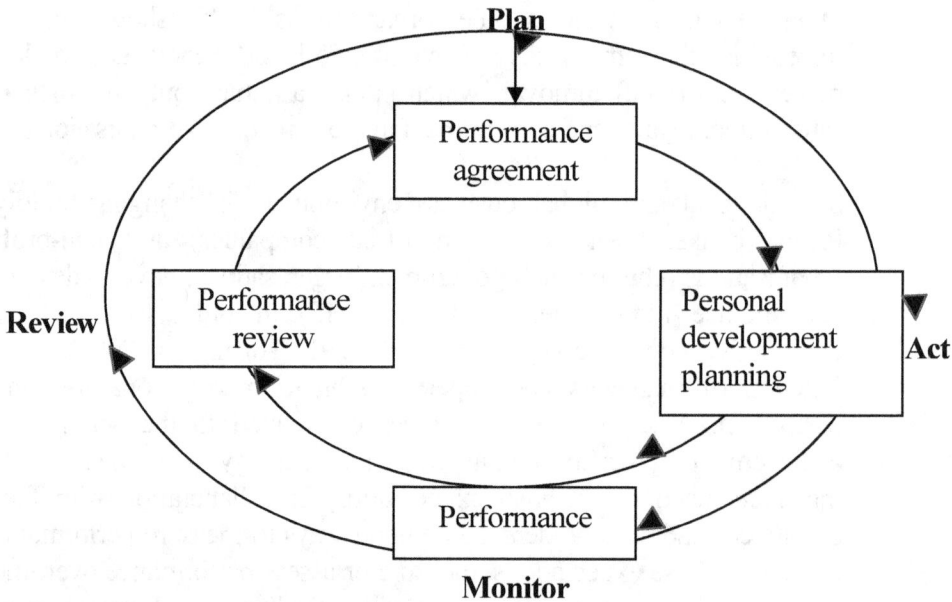

Figure 6.1 summarises the performance management cycle (Armstrong, 2006). Indeed, PM is concerned with measuring outputs in the shape of delivered performance compared with expectations expressed as objectives. Hence, PM focuses on targets, standards and performance measures or indicators; it is concerned with inputs and values that focus on future performance planning and improvement rather than on retrospective performance appraisal (Rothwell and Kazanas,

2004). So, PM is a cyclical process which aims at improving performance, e.g., the achievement of business targets and PM objectives which involves a measurement process, appraisal process with activities, implementation process with activities and monitoring process (Performance Management, 2009).

Accordingly, the purpose of PM is to improve team performance, based on the principles of measurement; appraisal; action and monitoring. However, PMS can be manifest in different forms depending on whether the aim is to further improve good performers, or deal with underperformance which can be applied to individuals, teams, groups or organisations.

Armstrong (2006, p. 2) has identified several aims of PM as expressed by various organisations:

> "1. Empowering, motivating and rewarding employees to do their best;
> 2. Focusing employees' tasks on the right things and doing them right;
> 3. Managing and resourcing performance against agreed objectives;
> 4. All individuals being clear about what they need to achieve and the expected standards;
> 5. Maximizing the potential of individuals and teams to benefit themselves and the organization."

Therefore, performance management should also be linked with the following objectives: strategy regarding longer-term goals, integration concerning various aspects of the business, people management, and individuals and teams (Performance Management: An Overview, 2004). So, the human resources' impact on business performance cannot be ignored. Huselid et al. (2001) also present a seven-step process for embedding HR systems within a firm's overall strategy implementation and measuring its activities as compelling to line managers and CEOs.

Furthermore, Huselid (1995) comprehensively evaluated the links between systems of high performance work practices and firm performance. Results based on a national sample of nearly one thousand firms indicated that these practices have an economically and statistically significant impact on both intermediate employee outcomes (turnover and productivity) and short- and long-term measures of corporate financial performance. This also goes in line with the conclusions of Ulrich (1998) and Ulrich et al. (1979a; 1979 b).

Briefly, PM is related to the human resource management system within organisations. Therefore, PMS can be seen as a communications system designed to help employees succeed and requires active participation by employees (Beer, 1984; Beardwell, et al. 2001; Storey, 1992). Ulrich et al. (1997b) have explored the myths and realities about HR management, with new realities replacing the existing and outdated myths.

A) Concerns and Difficulties in PM

Performance management is a holistic process, bringing together many of the elements aiming at resulting in a successful practice of people management, including in particular learning and development (Performance Management: An Overview, 2004). On the other hand, concerns of performance management may include concerns with: outputs, outcomes, process and inputs; planning ahead to achieve future success; continuous improvement; concerns with continuous development; communication concerns; stakeholders concerns; and concern for fairness and transparency (Armstrong, 2006). More concerns can also be associated with the coexistence of the three constituencies: the manager, the employee and the organisation. This is in addition to coordinating the needs of each may cause other difficulties (De Cenzo and Robbins, 1996).

B) Performance Appraisals (PA): Definition, Standards and Barriers

Performance appraisals can be defined as a formal system for measuring, evaluating and reviewing performance. This includes the phase of the cycle of the annual PM which comprises the process of reviewing employee performance, setting new performance objectives, documenting the review, and oral feedback in the form of verbal review in a face-to-face meeting (Performance Appraisals, 2009). Accordingly, PA generally aims at:

> "1. Deciding whether an employee should receive rewards or
>   increases and its relative size

2. Identifying potential employees for the promotion
3. Helping managers for carrying out the leadership function
4. Motivating employees by providing feedback on performance
5. Giving employees a chance to express their ambitions, hopes
and concerns, thereby enhancing career development"

(Du Brin, 2003, p. 275)

Traditionally, the most popular and used appraisal standards include the annual confidential report (ACR), management by objective (MBO) and the appraisal interview. This results in both the employee and manager not having the complete picture; hence the 360-degree appraisal emerged. It is like a 360-degree circle or the idea of getting an all-around picture of our employee's performance (McCourt and Eldridge, 2003). But there are a few common appraisal errors that can be seen as barriers to quality PA, e.g., personality conflict, halo effect, tendency errors, me effect, first impression, and potential bias (Effective Performance Appraisal, 2005).

Performance Management: Good Practice Model

A. Key Area Results (KARs)

KARs refers to general areas of outcomes/outputs for which the department's role is responsible. KARs describes what is expected from a member of the organisation in his/her role. They focus attention on actions and activities that will assist units and ultimately the department in performing effectively.

The primary tool for capturing KARs is a clear and concise work plan. It describes KARs and the criteria for measuring them. KARs is described together with the criteria by which they will be measured, the more effective the PM process will be (Senior Management Service, 2003). The identification of KARs covers many different aspects of the work the individual is responsible for: Specific tasks and events; expected performance levels; unique contribution and duties and support given by specialists (Senior Management Service, 2003).

The setting of KARs should be derived directly from the required outputs of the approved strategic/operational plan. KARs should be broken down into specific activities or outputs in a work plan.

Indicators are then used to indicate how the successful performance/ achievement of the activities or outputs will be measured.

Briefly, KARs should not simply be a repetition of the outputs of the persons under his/her control or the consultants to be contracted, but should where possible indicate the value to be added by the member.

B. Behaviour-Based Measures

Behaviour-based performance appraisal systems combine the best features such as goal-setting procedures, critical-incident methods and behaviour-based appraisals of various appraisal methods. Behaviour-based systems attempt to discern what a person does and know. In a behaviour-based system, PA is an on-going process of daily coaching, counselling and motivating employees to peak performance. Briefly, the basic steps to follow for developing a behaviour-based appraisal system include:

1. Establishing the essential job tasks and the essential knowledge, skills, abilities and (other personal) characteristics (KSACs) required for performing the job
2. Achieving general job categories or 'key elements' by grouping these job tasks and corresponding KSACs
3. Defining the performance standard for each key element from a behaviour viewpoint
4. Establishing a rating scale for evaluating employee performance against the performance standards
5. Organising the performance standards and rating-scale behavioural examples into a performance standards 'packet' and give it to all supervisors and employees
6. Creating a form to document employee performance in relation to the performance standards
7. Training all supervisors in the purpose and use of the performance standards and the performance-appraisal system
8. Reviewing continuously the appraisal process to make sure changing job conditions are reflected (Solie, 2006).

However, a weakness of such measurement tool is that many traits that are often considered to be related to good performance may not in fact have a relationship with performance.

C. Ongoing Feedbacks, Peer Evaluation and 360-Degree Appraisals

Feedback is a process by which effective performance is reinforced and less-than-desirable performance is corrected. Feedback is information that highlights the relationship between what is expected and what has been accomplished after the work is performed or the action is taken. McGill and Beatty (1992) provide useful suggestions about giving effective feedback, including clarity, emphasising the positive, being specific, focussing on behaviour rather than the person, referring to behaviour that can be changed. In other words, feedback should be descriptive rather than evaluative and owning the feedback.

Figure 6.2: 360-Degree Feedback

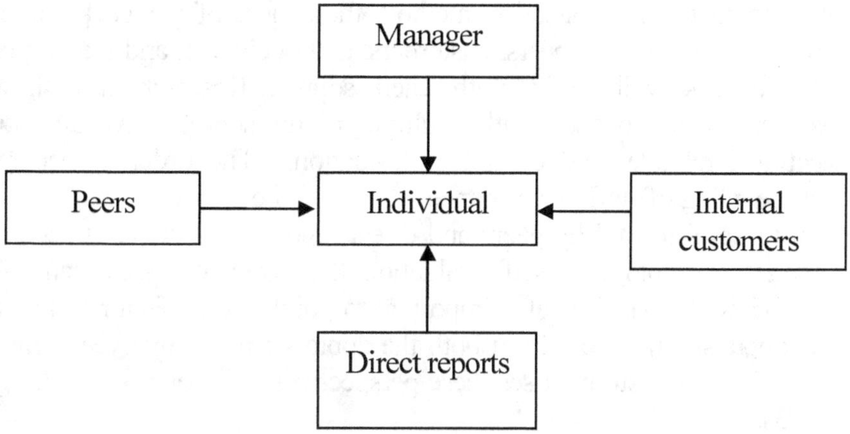

Moreover, Armstrong (2006, p.158) emphasised on the 360-degree feedback because according to a survey, only 30% of organisations in the survey used this approach. Figure 6.2 is a basic model for the 360-degree feedback.

Table 6.1: Appraiser and Appraisee Perspectives

	What does the Appraisee Know?	**What may Appraisee Not Know?**
What Appraiser Knows	• Personal data of individual • Current responsibilities • Outcomes of joint performance discussion as work proceeds	• Future work plans • Who is to be promoted • Emergent organisational perspectives
What Appraiser may Not Know	• Work aspects that satisfy/dissatisfy appraisee • Personal viwes on achievements/failures • Career ambitions • Development needs	• Capacity for specific roles • Development options available • Views of other colleagues on performance

According to this evaluation method, the sphere of feedback sources consists of managers, peers, customers, and one's self, and the purpose of feedback will differ with each source. Research has shown assessment approaches with multiple rating sources provide more accurate, reliable, and credible information. The order of accurate source rating of staff performance starts with the boss or manager of an employee, followed by peers and direct reports, and the least accurate being the employee's self evaluation (360-Degree Assessment: An Overview, 1997). It is also important to point out the factors affecting the appraisal interview from both the appraiser and employee point of view, Table 6.1 summarises these perspectives (McCourt and Eldridge, 2003).

D. Positive Reinforcement: Incentives and Rewards

Performance-driven organisations seek to create reward systems that not only link employee contributions to organisational results but also align closely with the organisation's strategic goals. The incentives and rewards system are used for motivation and recognition of high performance (Sharpley, 2002).

Rewards can take many forms as merit increases, bonuses, promotions, and other non-financial rewards. Likewise, the opportunity for greater rewards motivates employees to improve their performance and strive for greater achievements, which Stiffler (2006) describes as 'incentives driven performance'. Accordingly, performance management is about developing people and rewarding them in the broadest sense. Therefore, approaches to using performance management for non-financial rewards may include the combination of PM and recognition of people's achievements, provisions of opportunities to achieve, staff development, career planning, job engagement, and commitment (Armstrong, 2006).

Many organisations are aware that compensation helps drive individual and overall performance, but they struggle to consistently connect pay with performance. Therefore, the result is a mixed message to employees, de-motivating some and reinforcing the status quo with others. Therefore, a business can plan an effective incentive scheme in many ways along the following lines:

- Emphasising the importance of the scheme by allocating awards at annual intervals
- Simplifying the assessment process by setting specific categories for measuring performance
- Identifying key skills to decide who is eligible
- Setting benchmarks to track how people are performing
- Working out the best way to announce the reward
- Avoiding personalised awards (How to Reward People Effectively, 2002).

This can be realised by aligning behaviours with business objectives and appropriately leveraging incentives as well as organisations drive the types of activities that result in having a competitive advantage, profitability, and shareholder value (Barney, 1986 and 1991).

E. Trained Appraisers

Performance appraisals are efficient tools to develop staff and maximise their potential. Organisations do so through the training of managers and supervisors in conducting effective staff-evaluations. In a performance appraisals process, it is important that all staff is trained in supervision and appraisal processes. This is to be clear about what is expected of them and can benefit fully from the process. Accordingly, managers and staff must be trained to give and receive constructive feedback, respectively. Supervision, appraisal training and support should be available in a variety of delivery formats, e.g. classroom, online, telephone coaching and peer-to-peer discussion (Supervision and Appraisal, 2004). Therefore, training usually comprises both an understanding of the scheme and its objectives as well as training in the skills required (Appraisal Scheme, 2004).

In short, a theoretical good practice model for performance management systems is suitable to be adopted in many organisations such as banks and other profit-driven organisations as well as non profit organisations such as government bodies, ministries and educational institutions in Oman. In so doing, the current situation of performance management and current practices in the banks and other sectors should be evaluated leading to staff empowerment and continuous improvement or development.

Performance Management and Good Practice in Banks and other Organisations in Oman

Banks as well as profit-driven and non-profit organisations in Oman need to start their performance management systems with the following objectives by setting up:
1. a measurement process with activities
2. an appraisal process with activities
3. an implementation process with activities
4. a monitoring process with activities

Performance measures that are used as a management tool need to be broadened to include input and process measures. One approach is to use performance appraisals (PA) along with psychometric and behavioural tests could be a good initiative for a concern trying to rope in PMS as a means of improving its efficiency.

For the team performance, a team appraisal matrix can be utilised in which team members are listed on a vertical dimension, and specific tasks on the horizontal. Such an arrangement re-elects individual performance, and collectively reflects the overall team performance (Performance Appraisal, 1997).

1 Benefits of 'Good Practice' Model to the Banks and Other Organisations

Benefits are manifold, which comprise the emergence of good leadership, improvement of transparency across the organisation, emergence of efficient employees, provision of a happy employee-management relationship, identification of areas that need attention, and encouraging a healthy competition among employees.

Briefly, performance management is usually related to the human resource management system within organisations. Therefore, PMS can be seen as a communications system designed to help employees succeed and it requires active participation by employees.

2. Requirements to Adapt 'Good Practice' Model

Standard Chartered Bank, and other banks as well as many private and public sector organisations claim that they are using the 360-degrees appraisal. Their theoretical application of using the 'Good Practice' model can be a result of the barriers/absence of the conditions mentioned above. In fact, such a recommended model could also be a one-to-one discussion on the comments from the employee and the supervisor. Final comments of both the employee and the supervisor can then be recorded on the appraisal form. This will lead to transparency (as stated in the QA report, Lontok, 2009) and greater trust among the employees, which will help the organisation in long run.

3. Roles of Job Evaluation and Motivation in Performance Management

Evaluation of job and motivation are the key areas in PM. Assigning a job that an employee is incompetent to perform and then measure his/her performance against that job could lead to misleading conclusions about his performance. This could also account for lack of motivation. Thus, identifying the potential and allocating a job as per the potential of an employee will not only enhance the organisation's performance, but also help to sustain motivation among employees. Therefore, banks and other organisations should also explore the possibility of evaluating the job before allocation.

Conclusions and Recommendations

PMS is essential for any competitive organisation to achieve greater efficacy and brand leadership. The good practice model of PMS along with PA (360-degree appraisal) can be effectively adopted by the banks in the first phase. Its adaptability can be modified later as per the requirements.

Adopting and adapting performance management systems has become a necessity in the changing business world to meet global competition, even between non-profit organisations. PMS is a cyclical process aimed at improving performance continually. PM should be linked with two goals: strategic dealing with long-term goals, integrated concerning various aspects of the business, people management, and individuals and teams. The key to implementing an effective PMS is to identify day-to day hassles that executives go through.

In order to ensure sound HRM, HRD, staff empowerment, good performance meeting specified standards, as well as staff loyalty and commitment recommendations, performance appraisals are divided into two main categories:

- The need to adopt a good practice performance management model
- An effective performance appraisal standard

First, the adaptation of a sound good practice PM calls for the implementation of the natural process of management which comprises planning, acting, monitoring and reviewing, see Figure 6.1 above (Armstrong, 2006). Figure 6.3 also presents Armstrong's model (2006) for non-profit organisations which seems suitable for the banks and profit-driven and non-profit organisations for implementation.

Figure 6.3: Armstrong's Model for Non-Profit Organisations

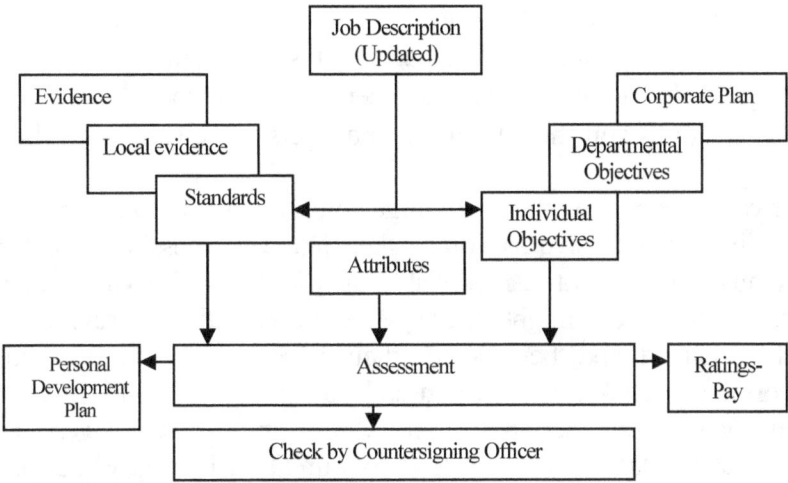

Second, it is highly recommended that management sincerely introduces contemporary systems that are being increasingly used such as the 360-degree appraisal and feedback system and face-to-face evaluation discussion through an interview. However, it is important to emphasise on the importance of training in this stage, and in this case it is the appraiser training on conducting an effective and fair evaluation. This is because evidence indicated that training appraisers can make them better raters or assessors and reduces or eliminates common errors or barriers that were mentioned earlier in the report such as the halo and leniency. After all, "poor appraisal is worse than no appraiser at all" (De Cenzo and Robbins, 1996, p. 343). Briefly, an efficient appraisal system cannot be without the following major components: transparency, feedback, coaching, promotion, rewards, and keeping individuals and teams motivated. In so doing, the short- and long-term strategic plans and objectives can be achieved as staff and managers are empowered, motivated, well-trained and appreciated. This should result in having pride in the bank or organisation as well as being loyal and committed to his/her organisation, as goals are aligned which is the basic foundation for the organisation to enjoy having a competitive edge.

Staff Appraisal: Organisation's and Managers' Roles

Organisations and managers should find answers to the following questions to secure a positive, constructive and a user-friendly mechanism for staff appraisal:

- Why performance management is important
- How to set up a workable performance management system
- Why you should evaluate managers as well as line workers

If you have ever worked for a large corporation, you can probably recall feeling apprehensive as you walked into your boss's office for your annual review. You can probably also identify with your employees' fears that they might leave your office after a review feeling disappointed and bewildered, their raises up in smoke and their confidence shaken. Thus you and your staff may think of employee evaluations as a necessary evil. Armstrong (2006) suggests a more palatable alternative. Instead of traditional, yearly performance appraisals, we also advocate performance management, a user-friendly system that emphasises collaboration between manager and employee. If you plan and execute it properly, performance management can help you monitor and encourage employee development over the long term, and avoid the unpleasant, confrontational experience of an annual evaluation.

References

360-Degree Assessment: An Overview. (1997), Available at:
http://www.opm.gov/perform/wppdf/360asess.pdf (Accessed on
9 November 2009).

Al Lamki, Salma M. (2005), "The Role of the Private Sector in
Omanization: The Case of the Banking Industry in the
Sultanate of Oman", *International Journal of Management*,
22, 2 June 2005, p.176.

Appraisal Scheme (2004), Available at: http://www.bcftcs.ac.uk/pdf/
SH-Appraisal.pdf (Accessed on 9 November 2009).

Armstrong, M. (2006), *Performance Management Key Strategies and
Practical Guidelines*, London, Institute of Personnel and
Development.

Armstrong, M and Baron, A (1998), *Performance Management: The
New Realities*, London, Institute of Personnel and
Development.

Bank Muscat (2006), Annual Report Annual Report, accessed on Nov
12, 2008,
http://www.bankmuscat.com/pdf/AnnualReport_2006.pdf.

Barney, J.B. (1986), "Organizational Culture: Can it be the Source of Sustained
Competitive Advantage," *Academy Management Review*, 11, 3, pp.
656-665.

Barney, J.B. (1991), "Firm Resources and Sustained Competitive Advantage,"
Journal of Management, 17, 1, pp. 99-120.

Beardwell, I *et al.* (2001), *Human Resource Management: A Contemporary
Approach*, 4th edition, Harlow, Financial Times/Prentice Hall.

Beer, M *et al.* (1984), *Managing Human Assets*, New York, Free Press.

Bratton, John and Gold, Jeffrey (2003), *Human Resource Management,-
Theory and Practice*, New York, Palgrave Macmillan.

Burns, N and Grove, SK. (1993), "The practice of nursing research. Conduct, critique and utilization", 2nd Edition, Philadelphia: W.B. Saunders Company.

Burns, N and Grove, SK. (2003), "Understanding nursing research", 3rd Edition. Philadelphia: W.B. Saunders Company.

Bergstrom Andreas, Ternehäll Mattias (2005), "Work Motivation in Banks", MBA thesis dated: 2005-06-02, Internat Ionel La Handel Shögskolan, Högskolan I Jönköping, English version available at: http://urn.kb.se/resolve?urn=urn:nbn:se:hj:diva-142.

CBO Annual Report (2007), available at http://www.cbo-oman.org, accessed on 11-08-08.

Cokins, Gary (2006), *Case Studies in Performance Management - A Guide from the Experts*, edited By Tony Adkins, New York, Wiley.

De Cenzo, D. and Robbins, S. (1996), *Human Resource Management*, 5th edition, Chichester, John Wiley and Sons.

Dick, Grote (2002), "Appraisal Question and Answer Book - A Survival Guide for Managers", *American Management Association*, p. 19.

Economist Intelligence Unit, Country Data (2006), EIU reports - Oman, available at http://www.eiu.com, accessed on 15-08-08

Effective Performance Appraisal (2005), Available at: http://hr.ag.ohio-state.edu/county_directors/GS9_Performance_Appraisal.pdf (Accessed on 8 November 2009).

EIU reports (2006), *Oman*, available at <http://www.eiu.com>, accessed on 15-08-08.

Fombrun, C.J. et al. (1984), *Strategic Human Resource Management*", New York, Wiley.

GCC Statistical Department (2005), Statistical Bulletin, through: http://www.gcc-sg.org/gccstatvol12/EcoStat/eco76.htm, accessed on 12-08-08.

Grote, Dick (2002), *Appraisal Question and Answer Book: A Survival Guide For Managers*, American Management Association.

Hofstede, Geert (1983), "National Cultures in Four Dimensions: A Research-Based Theory of Cultural Differences among Nations," *International Studies of Management and Organization*, Spring/ Summer, pp. 46-74.

Hunter, Larry W. and Thatcher, Sherry M. B. (2007), "Feeling the Heat: Effects of Stress, Commitment, and Job Experience on Job Performance", *Academy of Management Journal*, 50, 4, p. 953.

Huselid, M.A. (1995), The Impact of Human Resource Management Practices on Turnover, Productivity, and Corporate Financial Performance, *The Academy of Management Journal*, 38, 3, pp. 635-672.

Huselid, M.A., Ulrich, D. and Becker, B. E. (2001), *The HR Scorecard: Linking People, Strategy, and Performance*, Boston, Harvard Business School Press.

IRS (2007), *Employment Trends*, Aug, 2003 issue, pp. 1-11.

Lavender, Mark (2004), "Maximising customer relationships and minimising business risk", *The International Journal of Bank Marketing*, 22 No. 4, p. 291.

Lockett, J (1992) "Effective Performance Management", London, Kogan Page.

Lontok, Rolando Jr. (2009), Nizwah College: Report on the Quality Assurance Department (QAD) Formal Visit on 25 and 26 October 2009, Ministry of Manpower, Oman

Kelliny, W. (ed.) (1996), *Contemporary Education: Special Issue on Applied Linguistics and Research Inquiry, 40, 1, pp. 131-146.*

Kelliny, W. (2002), *Surveys in Linguistics and Language Teaching III: E-Learning and E-Research, New York, Peter Lang.*

Kelliny, W. (2010), *Marketing and Human Resources across Cultures*, Business and Economic Series, Volume 1, Seattle/Washington.

Kelliny, W. and Al Rizeiqi, Saleem S. (2011), *Perceptions of Organisations, Trainers and Employees of the Labour Market Needs and Wants*, Business and Economic Series, Volume 2, Seattle/Washington.

Kinnie, N. (2006), *A Presentation on HRM Issues in Service Sector*, www.people.bath.ac.uk/mnsnjk/HRM%20in%20the%20SS/introd uction%20to%20ss.ppt, accessed on 12-08-2008.

Mathis, Robert L. Jackson, John H. (2005), *Human Resource Management*, 9th ed., New York, Thomson Business and Professional Publishing.

McCourt, W. and Eldridge, D. (2003), *Global Human Resource Management: Managing People in Developing and Transitional Countries*, London, Edward Elgar.

McGill, I. and Beatty, L. (1992), *Action Learning: A Practitioner's Guide*, London, 2nd. Revised edition, London, Rutledge Falmer.

Ministry of Information (2001), *Oman Years of Achievement*, Muscat, Ministry of Information Press.

Ministry of National Economy (2006), *The Statistical Yearbook*, Oman, Ministry of National Economy.

Mohrman, A.M. and Mohrman, S A (1995), "Performance Management is 'Running the Business', *Compensation and Benefits Review*, July–August, pp 69–75.

Nickols, F. (2003), *Factors Affecting Performance. Distance Consulting*, http://home.att.net/nickols/articles.htm, accessed on 12-08-2008.

Oman Statistical Report (2006), Ministry of Information, through: www.omantel.om, accessed on 01-08-08.

Performance Appraisal (1997), Available at: http://filebox.vt.edu/users/dgc2/staffinghandbook/perfappraisal.htm (Accessed on 8 November 2009).

Performance Appraisals (2009), Available at:
  http://www.businessballs.com/performanceappraisals.htm (Accessed
  8 November 2009).
Performance Management (2009), Available at:
  http://www.teamtechnology.co.uk/performancemanagement.html
  (Accessed on 10 November 2009).

Performance Management: An Overview (2004), Available at:
  http://www.cipd.co.uk/subjects/perfmangmt/general/perfman.htm
  (Accessed on 18 November 2009).

Robert, C. et al. (2000), "Empowerment and Continuous Improvement
  in the United States, Mexico, Poland and India: Predicting Fit
  on the Basis of the Dimensions of Power Distance and
  Individualism," *Journal of Applied Psychology*, 85, 5, pp. 643-
  658.

Robert, C et al. (2005), *Human Resource Management*, New York,
  Thomson Business and Professional Publishing, pp. 73-80.

Rothwell, William J. and Kazanas, H. C. (2004), *Planning And
  Managing Human Resources Strategic Planning For Human
  Resources Management*, 2nd ed., Massachusetts, Press
  Amherst.

Schwepker, Charles H Jr. and Good, David J.(2004) "Marketing Control
  and Sales Force Customer Orientation," *Journal of Personal
  Selling and Sales Management*, 24, 3, pp. 167-168.

Senior Management Service (2003), Available at:
  http://www.dpsa.gov.za/documents/sms/publications/smshb2003.pdf
  (Accessed on 9 November 2009).

Sharpley, D. (2002) "Perceptions, motivation and performance", *DSA
  Business Psychology*, pp. 180-185.

Smith, Kirk et al. (2000), "Managing Salesperson Motivation in
  Territory Realignment", *Journal of Personal Selling and Sales
  Management*, 20, 4, p. 215.

Solie, C. (2009), Performance Appraisals. Available at: http://www.pei-
  911.com/HTML/article-performance.pdf (Accessed on 8 November
  2009).

Stiffler, M. (2006), *Incentive Compensation Management: Making Pay-for-Performance a Reality* (An Article by Mark Stiffler, Founder, President and CEO of Syngy, Inc.).

Storey, J. (1992), *Developments in the Management of Human Resources*, Blackwell, Oxford University Press.

Storey, J. (1992), *Developments in the Management of Human Resources*, Blackwell, Oxford University Press.

Supervision and Appraisal (2004), Available at: http://www.nta.nhs.uk/publications/DOCS/supervision.pdf (Accessed on 19 November 2009).

Torrington, D. et al. (2005), *Human Resource Management,* 6th edition, Harlow, Financial Times/Prentice Hall.

Ulrich, D., et al. (1997a) (ed.), 'Measuring Human Resources: An Overview of Practice and a Prescription for Results' *Human Resources Management,* 36, 3, pp. 303-320.

Ulrich, D., et al. (1997b), *Role of Forthcoming HR, Tomorrow's HR Management,* Chichester, John Wiley and Sons.

Ulrich, D., et al. (1998), 'A New Mandate for Human Resources' *Harvard Business Review,* 76, 1, pp. 124-134.

Whitaker, Debbie (2007), "Human Capital: Management or Measurement?", *Personnel Today*, 2, 13.

Wilkinson, A. (1995), "Towards HRM? A Case Study from Banking", *Research and Practice in Human Resource Management*, 31, pp. 97-115.

William, et al. (2003), Planning and Managing Human Resources Strategic Planning For Human Resources Management, 2nd ed., Massachusetts, Press Amherst.

Appendix A
A Questionnaire for Banking Staff

Dear colleague,

Thank you for participating in this research projects. You will find below a series of descriptions concerning 'the factors affecting performance of banking staff'. Please, mark the extent to which you agree or disagree with these statements.

Please, note that:

- The collected data will be used collectively for research purposes only
- The name of your organisation or employer will not be mentioned, as responses will be treated collectively.
- Confidentiality of responses, personal data or views will be kept and these will be used collectively for research purposes only.
- There is no right or wrong answer

So, please, just describe what you think and you feel as it is. We guarantee that your answers and personal data will be kept confidential.

Thank you in advance for your help and support.

The Research Team

1. What is your age category?

<20 years	1
20 - 29 years	2
30 - 39 years	3
40 - 49 years	4
50 - 59 years	5
More than 59	6

2. What is your gender?

Female	1
Male	2

3. What is your highest qualification?

Diploma in Banking	1
BBA in banking or similar	2
Postgraduate/ diploma in banking or similar	3
Bachelor's degree	4
Master's degree	5
Doctoral degree	6
Other: _____	7

4. How many years have you been in banking?

0 - 5 years	1
6 -10 years	2
11- 15 years	3
16 -20 years	4
More than 20 years	5

5.   In which type of bank are you currently employed?

Private	1
Public	2
Public-central	3
Foreign	4
Specialised	5

6. What is your current employment status in this bank?

Full-time	1
Part-time	2
Other_____	3

7. In what type of department are you currently allocated?

Cash	1
Accounts	2
HRM	3
IT	4
Deposits	5
Loan/allied services	6
Operations	7
Other_____	8

8. Indicate how long you have been working in this department:

0 - 12 months	1
1 - 2 years	2
2 - 3 years	3
3 - 4 years	4
5 years and longer	5

9. Indicate how you regard your knowledge and skills in your current job position by circling appropriate number (only one) against the category.

1. Very poor, 2. Poor, 3. Average, 4. Good, 5. Excellent

No.	Statement	1	2	3	4	5
1	Planning of bank everyday activities					
2	Implementing plans					
3	Assessment of customer requirement					
4	Implementing of banking performance standards					
5	Knowledge in accounts/finance current affairs					
6	Banking competencies					
7	Interpersonal relations					
8	Customer counselling skills					

1. Very poor, 2. Poor, 3. Average, 4. Good, 5. Excellent

No.	Statement	1	2	3	4	5
9	Self assessment with regard to outcome of performance					
10	Supervision of customer care					
11	Supervising trainee					
12	In-service training	12	12	12	12	12
13	Management of time	13	13	13	13	13
14	Improvement of quality of care	14	14	14	14	14
15	Maintaining facilities, equipment and supplies	15	15	15	15	15

10. Out of the tasks described in earlier sections, which one you find the most difficult and why?

....

....

....

11. Please indicate up to two other important competencies or skills you wish to acquire in your current position.

....

....

....

12. How is performance reviewed in your organization for various categories of employees? Circle only one.

A formal system of regular appraisals with reviews of past performance, setting of objectives	1
Informal, but regular reviews involving discussions about past performance and agreed actions for the future.	2
Informal, *ad hoc* reviews, undertaken especially when there is a performance problem	3
Not reviewed	4

13. If you have a performance appraisal system in place, how are the results of the performance appraisal utilised?

Training	1
Promotion	2
Demotion	3
Rotation	4
Not used	5

14. Please answer the following questions about performance appraisal and utilisation by circling appropriate number (only one) against the categories:

1 = Strongly disagree; 2 = Disagree; 3 = Uncertain; 4 = Agree;
5 = Strongly agree.

No.	Statement	1	2	3	4	5
1	Objectives to be achieved are known by individuals to be assessed					
2	Performance standards expected from staff are clear and understood by all					
3	Constructive feedback on performance appraisal results is provided on a regular basis					
4	Feedback of how staff is performing is provided throughout the year					
5	Prompt action is taken when performance falls below acceptable standards					
6	My managers/supervisor inspires me to do my best					
7	Staff are given opportunity to make comments on the results of their performance					

15. Now answer the following questions on remuneration, benefits and recognition.

1 = Strongly disagree; 2 = Disagree; 3 = Uncertain; 4 = Agree;
5 = Strongly agree

No.	Statement	1	2	3	4	5
1	Your remuneration is competitive compared to other similar organizations.					
2	Remuneration is in accordance with your experience.					
3	Remuneration is in accordance with your job responsibility					
4	Fringe benefits are known to you					
5	You are satisfied with your fringe benefits.					
6	Opportunities exist for career advancement.					
7	Hardworking are recognised.					

16. Would you like to comment on these in Q15?

....
....
....
....

17. Now answer regarding your staffing work scheduling:

1 = Strongly disagree; 2 = Disagree; 3 = Uncertain; 4 = Agree;
5 = Strongly agree

No.	Statement	1	2	3	4	5
1	You get opportunities to make inputs into staffing policies and procedures					
2	Opportunities exist for a flexible work schedule					
3	The overall work schedule is fair					
4	Overtime work is acceptable.					
5	There is a good balance between people who supervise work and people who do the work.					
6	The allocated staff in my unit is sufficient to cover the current workload.					
7	Care and support of staff in the form of counselling at the workplace is available.					

18. Now answer regarding staff development:

1 = Strongly disagree; 2 = Disagree; 3 = Uncertain; 4 = Agree;
5 = Strongly agree

No.	Statement	1	2	3	4	5
1	Opportunities for advancing in the organization exist					
2	Good opportunities for continuing education are available.					
3	The necessary training is given to ensure job effectiveness.					
4	Job specific refresher courses are available.					
5	In-service training adequately addresses the skill gaps					
6	Incompetent staff are identified and provided with the necessary support.					
7	Good leadership/management training available.					
8.	Staff participates in identifying their staff development needs.					

19. Now regarding your workspace and environment:

1 = Strongly disagree; 2 = Disagree; 3 = Uncertain; 4 = Agree;
5 = Strongly agree

No.	Statement	1	2	3	4	5
1	My work environment is safe and free from hazards.					
2	Good workplace layout					
3	Comfortable temperature.					
4	Necessary instruments are available.					
5	Instruments in working conditions.					
6	Materials and supplies sufficient.					
7	Fire and safety protection is available .					
8.	Security from anti social elements in handling money is available.					

The following questions are related to confirmative statement. Give your perception honestly. According to the scales used in previous questions encircle the appropriate number:

1 = Strongly disagree; 2 = Disagree; 3 = Uncertain; 4 = Agree;
5 = Strongly agree

No.	Statement	1	2	3	4	5
20	I work with skilled competent people who are good at their jobs					
21	My performance is judged more by how much work I do than by how well I do it					
22	I find my work rewarding					
23	I am afraid to openly express my ideas and opinions					
24	People in this organization have a shared sense of purpose					
25	Doing this job makes me feel good about myself					
26	I am subject to personal criticism and abuse					
27	People in this organization put more energy into identifying mistakes than into figuring out how to do things right					
28	I do not like the way the organization operates					
29	The way things are organised around here makes it hard for people to do their best work.					
30	I am proud to tell people that I work for this organization					
31	Some cultural believes in the community I am living is in conflict with some of my organization's policies					
32	I am not included in activities or made to feel part of the team					
33	am constantly seeking out new challenges at work					
34	The community I live in has the highest regards for my organization					
35	In this organization, people in different departments or programmes try to help each other.					
36	Most people here know how their work contributes to this organization's mission.					
36	I receive prompt acknowledgement and recognition for doing a good job.					

1 = Strongly disagree; 2 = Disagree; 3 = Uncertain; 4 = Agree;
5 = Strongly agree

No.	Statement	1	2	3	4	5
38	My manager/supervisor inspires me to do my best.					
39	Judgement about my performance is fair.					
40	This organization's mission is understood by everyone who works here					
41	The people I work with are comfortable in suggesting changes and improvements to each other.					
42	Senior managers in this organization are open to new ideas and suggestions.					
43	I am clear about the objectives I need to achieve.					
44	I trust and respect my immediate supervisor.					
45	My manager emphasises my positive contributions when reviewing my performance					
46	When changes are made in the way things are done, management always first informs the people who will be affected.					
47	There is a great deal of cooperation between people in this organization.					
48	When I retire I will receive a reasonable pension from this organization.					
49	I am given enough authority to allow me to do my job effectively.					
50	If I have an idea for improving the way we do our work, my supervisor/manager will usually listen to me.					
51	I feel my work contributes to the organization's performance.					
52	The work I do gives me a feeling of personal achievement.					
53	My pay is competitive to other, similar organizations.					
54	My colleagues value my contribution.					
55	My manager/supervisor gives me regular, timely feedback that helps me improve my performance					
56	This organization provides me with skills and knowledge that will benefit my future career.					

57. What are the things you most like about working for this organization?

....
....
....
....
....
....

58. What are the things you like least?

....
....
....
....
....

59. What would you most like to see changed/improved? (And any other relevant comments)

....
....
....
....
....

Thank you very much for spending time to answer the questionnaire

The Research Team

Appendix B
A Questionnaire for Banking Managers

Dear Sir, Madam,

Thank you for participating in this research projects. You will find below a series of descriptions concerning 'the factors affecting performance of banking staff'. Please, mark the extent to which you agree or disagree with these statements.

Please, note that:

- The collected data will be used collectively for research purposes only
- The name of your organisation or employer will not be mentioned, as responses will be treated collectively.
- Confidentiality of responses, personal data or views will be kept and these will be used collectively for research purposes only.
- There is no right or wrong answer

So, please, just describe what you think and you feel as it is. We guarantee that your answers and personal data will be kept confidential.

Thank you in advance for your help and support.

The Research Team

1. What is your age category?

<20 years	1
20 - 29 years	2
30 - 39 years	3
40 - 49 years	4
50 - 59 years	5
More than 59 years	6

2. What is your gender?

Female	1
Male	2

3. What is your highest qualification?

Diploma in Banking	1
BBA in banking or similar	2
Postgraduate/diploma in banking or similar	3
Bachelor's degree (BA)	4
Master's degree	5
Doctoral degree	6
Other: ………………………………	7

4. How many years have you been in banking?

0 - 5 years	1
6 -10 years	2
11- 15 years	3
16 -20 years	4
More than 20 years	5

4. In which type of bank are you currently employed?

Private	1
Public	2
Public-central	3
Foreign	4
Specialised	5

5. What is your current employment status in this bank?

Full-time	1
Part-time	2
Other	3

7. Have you as a manager been involved with any of the following? Answer either NO (1) or YES (2) for each of the following.

No.	TASK	NO	YES
1.	Providing training to employees.		
2.	One-to-one performance interview related to performance outcome.		
3.	Placement of staff according to skills.		
4.	Orientation of new staff.		
5.	Managing conflict.		
6.	Operational research.		
7.	Counselling of employees.		

8. Which of these tasks did you find the most difficult and why?

....

....

....

9. Have you received any management training or training in specific
   aspects related to management?

No	**1**
Yes	**2**

I0. If you answered YES in question 9, please give the following particulars regarding management training or training in aspects related to management which you received. If your answer was NO in question 9, please go to question 11 (ignore question I0).

No.	Please indicate course(s) received and duration of course in days.	Year (s)
1		
2		
3		
4		

1 1 . Indicate how you regard your management skills for overseeing the effective functioning of the ward(s) under your supervision. Please indicate as follows:

1. Very poor, 2. Poor, 3. Average, 4. Good, 5. Excellent

No.	Statement	1	2	3	4	5
1						
2						
3						
4						
5						
6						
7						
8.						

	Level of Management Perception	1	2	3	4	5
No.	Knowledge/skills					
1.	Banking service policy implementation.					
2.	Planning banking service delivery.					
3.	Audit					
4.	Development of performance standards.					
5.	Development of competencies.					
6.	Skills development.					
7.	Interpersonal relations.					
8.	Counselling skills.					
9.	Performance appraisal of subordinates.					
10	Supportive supervision.					
11	Problem solving					
12	Motivation of staff.					
13	Organising facilities, equipment and supplies.					

12. How often or in which way is performance reviewed in your organisation for various categories of employees?

A formal system of regular appraisals with reviews of past performance and setting of	1
Informal, but regular reviews involving discussions about past performance and agreed	2
Informal, *ad hoc* reviews, undertaken especially when there is a performance problem.	3
Not reviewed.	4

I3. Indicate your response to the following questions regarding performance appraisal and utilisation in your organization or unit.

1 = Strongly disagree; 2 = Disagree; 3 = Uncertain; 4 = Agree; 5 = Strongly agree

No.	Statement	1	2	3	4	5
1	Objectives to be achieved are known by individuals to be assessed.					
2	One-to-one performance interview on the outcome of performance appraisal is conducted.					
3	Performance standards expected from staff are clear and understood by all.					
4	Peer review of performance is done.					
5	Constructive feedback on performance appraisal results is provided on a regular basis.					
6	Feedback of how staff is performing is provided throughout the year.					
7	Prompt action is taken when performance falls below acceptable standards.					
8.	Managers/supervisor inspires staff to do their best.					
9	Staff are given an opportunity to make comments on the results of their performance.					
10	Self assessment by employees to review their own performance is done.					

14. Please indicate your response to each of the following questions regarding your remuneration, benefits and recognition.

1 = Strongly disagree; 2 = Disagree; 3 = Uncertain; 4 = Agree;
5 = Strongly agree

No.	Statement	1	2	3	4	5
1	Your remuneration is competitive compared to other similar organizations.					
2	Remuneration is in accordance with your experience.					
3	Remuneration is in accordance with your job responsibility.					
4	Fringe benefits are known to you.					
5	You are satisfied with your fringe benefits.					
6	Opportunities exist for career advancement.					
7	The efforts of hardworking staff are recognized.					

I5. Would you like to comment on any of your responses in questionI4?

....
....
....
....
....
....
....
....
....
....

16. Please indicate your response to each of the following questions regarding staffing and work schedules.

1 = Strongly disagree; 2 = Disagree; 3 = Uncertain; 4 = Agree;
5 = Strongly agree

No.	Statement	1	2	3	4	5
1	You get opportunities to make inputs into staffing policies and procedures.					
2	Opportunities exist for a flexible work schedule.					
3	The overall work schedule is fair.					
4	Overtime work is acceptable.					
5	There is a good balance between people who supervise work and people who do the work.					
6	The allocated staff in my unit are sufficient to cover the current workload.					
7	Care and support of staff in the form of counselling at the workplace is available.					

17. Please indicate your response to each of the following regarding staff development. Please answer the statement according to your judgement

1 = Strongly disagree; 2 = Disagree; 3 = Uncertain; 4 = Agree;
5 = Strongly agree

No.	Statement	1	2	3	4	5
1	Opportunities for advancing in the organization exist.					
2	Good opportunities for continuing education are available.					
3	The necessary training is given to ensure job effectiveness.					
4	Job specific refresher courses are available.					
5	In-service training adequately addresses the skill gaps.					

1 = Strongly disagree; 2 = Disagree; 3 = Uncertain; 4 = Agree;
5 = Strongly agree

	Statement	1	2	3	4	5
6	Incompetent workers are identified and provided with the necessary support.					
7	Good leadership/management training is available.					
8.	Professional bankers participate in identifying their staff development needs.					

18. Please indicate your response to each of the following statements regarding workspace and environment.

1 = Strongly disagree; 2 = Disagree; 3 = Uncertain; 4 = Agree;
5 = Strongly agree

No.	Statement	1	2	3	4	5
1	My work environment is safe and free from hazards.					
2	Good workplace layout.					
3	Comfortable temperature.					
4	Necessary equipment are available.					
5	Equipment in working condition.					
6	Materials and supplies are sufficient.					
7	Wash room and other facilities are present					
8.	Cleanliness control strategy guidelines are available.					
9	Necessary policies are available.					

19. Indicate your response to each of the following statements with regard to management and leadership.

1 = Do not know; 2 = Do not agree; 3 = Tend to agree; 4 = Agree;
5 = Fully agree

No.	Statement	1	2	3	4
1	Leadership style is the way in which the management philosophy manifests itself in practice.				
2	The leadership style in our country over the last 20 years has been one of democratic leadership.				

1 = Do not know; 2 = Do not agree; 3 = Tend to agree; 4 = Agree;
5 = Fully agree

No.	Statement	1	2	3	4
3	Problem solving is more successful when managed immediately by the supervisor, rather than involving the specific subordinates.				
4	Managers should possess adequate communication skills.				
5	Due to the heavy work load of managers, it is not expected that they should have a training function.				
6	customer care is the primary function of the manager; therefore personnel management can be managed by the personnel department.				
7	Extrinsic motivation of employees involves stimulation of goal achievement.				
8.	Management's leadership style has an effect on the level of performance inclination.				
9	A position of authority is required in management positions to ensure successful influencing of subordinates.				
10	Traditionally, managers in Oman have had an autocratic style of management.				
11	Participative management involves shared decision- making.				
12	Employees, who receive frequent feedback concerning their performance, are usually more highly motivated than those who do not.				

Questions 20-56:

Please answer the statement according to your judgement.

1 = Strongly disagree; 2 = Disagree; 3 = Uncertain; 4 = Agree;
5 = Strongly agree

No.	Statement	1	2	3	4	5
20	I work with skilled competent people who are good at their jobs.					
21	My performance is judged more by how much work I do than by how well I do it.					
22	I find my work rewarding					
23	I am afraid to openly express my ideas and opinions.					
24	People in this organization have a shared sense of purpose.					
25	Doing this job makes me feel good about myself.					
26	I am subject to personal criticism and abuse					
27	People in this organization put more energy into identifying mistakes than into figuring out how to do things right.					
28	I do not like the way the organization operates					
29	The way things are organised around here makes it hard for people to do their best work.					
30	I am proud to tell people that I work for this organization.					
31	Some cultural believes in the community I am living is in conflict with some of my organization's policies.					
32	I am not included in activities or made to feel part of the team.					
33	I am constantly seeking out new challenges at work.					
34	The community I live in has the highest regards for my organization.					

1 = Strongly disagree; 2 = Disagree; 3 = Uncertain; 4 = Agree;
5 = Strongly agree

No.	Statement	1	2	3	4	5
35	In this organization, people in different departments or programmes try to help each other.					
36	Most people here know how their work contributes to this organization's mission.					
36	I receive prompt acknowledgement and recognition for doing a good job.					
38	My manager/supervisor inspires me to do my best.					
39	Judgement about my performance is fair					
40	This organization's mission is understood by everyone who works here.					
41	The people I work with are comfortable in suggesting changes and improvements to each other.					
42	Senior managers in this organization are open to new ideas and suggestions.					
43	I am clear about the objectives I need to achieve.					
44	I trust and respect my immediate supervisor.					
45	My manager emphasises my positive contributions when reviewing my performance.					
46	When changes are made in the way things are done, management always first informs the people who will be affected.					
47	There is a great deal of cooperation between people in this organization.					
48	When I retire I will receive a reasonable pension from this organization.					
49	I am given enough authority to allow me to do my job effectively.					

1 = Strongly disagree; 2 = Disagree; 3 = Uncertain; 4 = Agree;
5 = Strongly agree

No.	Statement	1	2	3	4	5
50	If I have an idea for improving the way we do our work, my supervisor/manager will usually listen to me.					
51	I feel my work contributes to the organization's performance.					
52	The work I do gives me a feeling of personal achievement.					
53	My pay is competitive to other, similar organizations.					
54	My colleagues value my contribution.					
55	My manager/supervisor gives me regular, timely feedback that helps me improve my performance					
56	This organization provides me with skills and knowledge that will benefit my future career.					

57. What are the things you most like about working for this organization?

....
....
....
....
....
....
....
....
....
....
....

58. What are the things you like least?

....
....
....
....
....
....
....
....
....
....
....

59. What would you most like to see changed/improved? (And any other relevant comments)

....
....
....
....
....
....
....
....
....
....
....

Thank you very much for spending time to answer the questionnaire

The Research Team

www.ingramcontent.com/pod-product-compliance
Lightning Source LLC
Chambersburg PA
CBHW081131170526
45165CB00008B/2634